500

quick meals

500
quick meals

the only compendium of quick meals you'll ever need

Deborah Gray

SELLERS
PUBLISHING

A Quintet Book

Published by Sellers Publishing, Inc.
161 John Roberts Road, South Portland, Maine 04106
Visit our Web site: www.sellerspublishing.com
E-mail: rsp@rsvp.com

ISBN: 978-1-4162-0882-2
Library of Congress Control Number: 2012941684
QTT.FHQM

This book was conceived, designed, and produced by
Quintet Publishing Limited
6 Blundell Street
London N7 9BH
United Kingdom

Food Stylist: Jayne Cross
Photographer: Jon Whitaker
Art Director: Michael Charles
Project Editor: Ross Fulton
Editorial Director: Donna Gregory
Publisher: Mark Searle

10 9 8 7 6 5 4 3 2 1

Printed in China by 1010 Printing International Ltd.

contents

introduction

This book is for those who appreciate good food, but are pressed for time; the emphasis is on creative, rather than complicated, dishes. Most of these recipes require only a few fresh ingredients, and the remaining items are familiar and easy to source. While I don't question the value of canned and frozen goods, which are a gift to the busy cook, they are used here in moderation and with discretion to exploit their value as a shortcut in a recipe, rather than as a meal substitute. All of the recipes can be prepared in half an hour or less, which is hardly any longer than a frozen dinner takes to heat through. Instead of a bland, salty, mass-produced flavor, you benefit from the fresh, bright palate of tastes found only in freshly cooked food.

The format of this book was devised for the busy cook; all the base recipes are clearly written and the instructions simple to follow. However, the variations give you plenty of other options which, with a few tweaks to the original recipe, can expand your repertoire of quick meal options. These ideas are not just here to be followed; they are intended to provide a starting point for a whole range of other ideas to suit your tastes and your diet.

The book is full of delicious recipes for all occasions, whether it's a sit-down dinner party, a few friends for an impromptu supper, or a hasty lunch for the family. There are comforting recipes (some with a novel quick-dish twist) and a selection of recipes that draw on international cuisines, contemporary palates, and the availability of so many exciting ingredients that you can now find in the supermarket.

Pasta Primavera, page 185

timing

It is nearly impossible to provide absolute timings in a cookbook; the time it takes to cut an onion is different for everyone. Similarly, different ovens cook differently and timings can vary significantly. For each recipe I provide an approximate cooking time that is intended as a guide: each main recipe features a clock icon in the upper left corner of the page which gives the estimated length of time required for preparing, cooking and serving, to the nearest five minute increment. This is a sixty minute timer rather than a twelve hour clock — these are quick meals after all, and no recipe takes longer than thirty minutes.

shopping hints for the speedy cook

The beauty of quick cooking is that the flavors are more intense than the mellower, gradual melding of flavors brought about by slow cooking. This means that the ingredients must be fresh, with an emphasis on quality.

meat and poultry
Quick-to-cook cuts of meat tend to be more expensive. The average portion size in the book is generally 4–6 ounces, but it is better to buy less than to compromise by buying cuts that need long cooking to tenderize, which will inevitably disappoint. Look for meat that has been prepared for stir-fries or ask the butcher to do this for you; this is a timesaver.

fish
Fish is a godsend for the fresh cook, since it's cooked in minutes. Buy prepared fillets when possible — timings in this book don't include the time it takes to fillet. Frozen fish and seafood are excellent, but need to be properly thawed before use.

vegetables
The vegetables in this book are mostly fresh, with the exception of peas and corn; however, if you wish to use frozen beans, spinach, bell pepper, or onions, go ahead. Similarly, with garlic or ginger, the recipes often call for minced garlic cloves or fresh ginger, but substituting prepared garlic or ginger paste is absolutely fine. You can buy prepared vegetables in the store if time is really short, but these are an expensive choice and save only a couple of minutes. The exceptions are packaged baby spinach that saves on repeated washing time, and mixed exotic stir-fry vegetables and mixed salad leaves, all of which save buying a number of different vegetables.

herbs

Many recipes ask for fresh chopped herbs. This is a harder one to compromise on, since dried herbs need time and liquid to rehydrate and release their flavors. An increasing range of frozen chopped herbs are available and make better substitutes. It actually requires little time to prepare your own; simply buy a big bunch of parsley, chop it in the food processor, and seal in a plastic tub or resealable bag before freezing. It is best to use herbs within three months of freezing them.

cheese

In general, use a well-flavored, sharp cheese for cooking; otherwise you will have to add a good deal more cheese to get any flavor in the finished dish. This is wasteful in monetary terms, but it also means you are cooking with more fat than necessary. The goat cheese used in this book is generally soft and comes in a log or a small round. Where ricotta or mascarpone cheeses are specified, cream cheese may be substituted. If you use low-fat cream cheese, remember that it is softer than its full-fat cousin so it may produce thinner results.

creams

Usually the lowest fat option has been given, but in desserts that call for cream to be whipped, heavy cream or whipping cream is a must. Soy cream may be substituted for half and half, and various low-fat cream substitutes may be used with discretion. Some recipes call for sour cream, but low-fat sour cream or crème frâiche may be used in its place.

preparation hints

check the recipe
Make sure that you have the ingredients you need to make the recipe, or you may spend ages pondering about substitutions or, worse, having to make a special visit to the store. Read the recipe first to get an idea of how to plan the preparation. For instance, in many recipes you can use the time while the onion is softening to chop the remaining ingredients; you don't have to do all the preparation before you begin to cook.

the right kit
Of all the fancy gadgets you can have on hand, nothing is better than a good-quality, sharp cook's knife. Wash it separately with care, sharpening it regularly, and it will last for years. Use a food processor with discretion; it can take longer to wash than it saves by chopping or shredding manually. For puréeing soups, a handheld immersion (stick) blender is most effective, as it can be used directly in the saucepan.

watching the pot
Unless specifically stated otherwise, most things just need the occasional stir and a watchful eye while they cook. Do proceed with other things such as making a salad, setting the table, and clearing the work surface when the cooking does not need your attention.

taste
Salt and pepper levels are left to your discretion as personal taste is most important here. The same goes for other spices such as chiles and sauces. If you know you like your food spicy, you can be liberal, but add little by little, tasting as you go if you are in any doubt. In quick cooking, what you taste is what you get — there is no time for flavors to mellow.

the essentials

The following is a list of the basics for a well-kept kitchen; it limits your creativity if you don't have the right ingredients at your fingertips. You will store more or less depending on space, but you will be able to make almost all the dishes in the book with these items.

the pantry

cans & jars
Beans — cannellini, black, pinto, and garbanzo beans are mainstays. Lentils are a handy standby.
Broth — cans of broth are time-saving additions to soups and the base for many sauces.
Capers — a bit of a luxury, but great for enlivening fish and pasta dishes.
Chipotle chiles — wonderful for spicing up a bland sauce.
Coconut milk — low-fat is best for health, but is thinner in flavor and texture.
Fruit — cans of peaches and pineapple. Cherries in jars are best. Use those fancy Christmas presents warmed and served with ice cream for an instant dessert.
Marinara sauce — a good-quality tomato-based sauce is great for creating a quick pasta or meat sauce; add fresh chopped herbs or a few teaspoons of pesto to reinvigorate.
Pesto — add to soups, sauces, and butter. Keep in the refrigerator after opening.
Preserves and honey — strawberry preserve, grape jelly, liquid honey.
Roasted peppers — a godsend. Other antipasti in a jar, such as artichokes, are also great.
Tomatoes — chopped are best, and one with Italian seasonings can be handy. Tomato sauce is great, particularly in soups; a tube of tomato paste is a must.
Tuna, salmon, sardines, anchovies, and other oily fish — perfect for sandwiches and a quick salad or starter. Choose water-packed fish to avoid unwanted fats.

dry goods

Chocolate — unsweetened cocoa powder, semisweet and white chocolate chips, and some good high cocoa-butter chocolate for indulgences.

Couscous and bulgur — couscous cooks in 5 minutes; some fancy flavored varieties are nice for a change with simple food. Bulgur takes longer to cook, but is still quicker than rice.

Flour — all-purpose flour is essential.

Mushrooms — dried mushrooms may take a bit of time to dehydrate, but they are intense in flavor and great when fresh are not on hand.

Noodles — egg and soba noodles cook very quickly.

Pasta — spaghetti, tagliatelle, penne, or a shaped variety.

Polenta — the quick-cook variety is ready in a few minutes; ready-made is fantastic for slicing and frying.

Pulses — red and puy (French green) lentils are the only pulses that cook relatively quickly.

Quinoa — a high-fiber protein that is great for salads and as a quick side.

Rice — quick-cook is the best. Brown rice is slow to cook, but if this is what you like, cook in bulk and freeze in portions. Basmati is good with Asian food.

Sugar — white, superfine, confectioners', and brown.

herbs & seasonings

Bay leaves

Bouillon cubes or powder — good-quality

Cayenne pepper

Chiles — whole

Chili — dried chili flakes

Cinnamon — ground and sticks

Coriander — ground

Cumin — ground

Curry powder — a good medium one
Garlic powder and paste
Ginger — ground and ginger paste
Herbs — dill, thyme, sage, mint, other dried herbs
Mustard — Dijon and whole-grain
Pepper — freshly ground black can't be beaten for taste; white for seasoning pale foods
Salt — sea salt has the best taste

liquid condiments & jars
Apple cider wine vinegar
Balsamic vinegar
Hoisin sauce
Hot sauce
Maple syrup
Mayonnaise
Olive oil
Soy sauce or tamari — preferably low-sodium
Sunflower or canola oil
Vanilla extract
Worcestershire sauce

dried fruit & nuts
Dried fruit — apricots, cranberries, pitted dates, raisins
Nuts — almonds, cashew, pecans, walnuts
Seeds — poppy, pumpkin, sesame, sunflower

the freezer

Bacon — slices or chopped lardons.

Bread and rolls — a good selection for sandwiches and accompaniments. Sliced bread can be toasted from frozen; leftover bread can be crumbed and stored in resealable plastic bags.

Fish and seafood — shrimp (shelled and deveined for speedy prep) and mixed seafood, frozen white fish and salmon fillets, packaged smoked salmon.

Fruit — frozen berries and apples for quick-fix crisps and pies.

Herbs — cilantro, basil, parsley.

Ice

Ice cream — at least vanilla and a selection of flavors for instant desserts.

Meat — a package of Parma or other air-dried ham, hamburger, chicken breasts.

Nuts — store in the freezer, not the pantry, to prevent the oils from turning rancid.

Pastry — puff, phyllo, prepared shells.

Vegetables — peas and corn. Optional: spinach, beans, bell peppers; sliced onions, shallots, garlic.

the refrigerator

Dairy — milk, yogurt, sour cream, butter (sweet, if only buying one); cheese: cheddar or Monterey Jack, blue cheese, goat cheese.

Eggs — large eggs are used in this book.

Fruit — lemons, limes, oranges, apples.

Salad goods — lettuce or mixed salad leaves, cucumber. (Tomatoes should be stored in a pantry as they lose their flavor when cold.)

Pickles — cornichons, chutney, dill pickles.

a few basic recipes

If you want to be prepared with a couple of recipe foundations, invest a little time in making a basic tomato sauce and a béchamel sauce, and freeze them. Then, a great pasta, meat, or fish dish or a mac and cheese will always be available at the drop of a hat without resorting to cans or packages. A basic chicken stock is also provided here, as it is such a shame to throw out chicken bones that could provide a delicious base for a soup on another day.

basic tomato sauce

A classic recipe used as a base for many stews, pasta sauces, and soups.

To serve 4 (makes 2 1/2 cups)	To make in bulk (10 cups)	
2 tbsp.	1/4 cup	olive oil
1 medium	2 large	onion, chopped
1 small	2 large	carrot, shredded
2 or 2 tsp.	8 or 2 1/2 tbsp.	medium garlic cloves, minced
1 (15-oz.)	2 (28-oz.)	canned chopped tomatoes, drained
2 tbsp.	1/2 cup	tomato paste
1/4 cup	1 cup	red wine or juice from the tomatoes
1 tsp.	4 tsp.	dried basil or oregano
		sea salt and black pepper

Heat the oil in a saucepan and add the onion and carrot. Cook gently over low heat until the onion is soft, 5–7 minutes. Add the garlic and cook for 1 minute, then stir in the remaining ingredients. Add salt and pepper to taste. Cook for 10 minutes, or until the sauce has thickened. The sauce may be left chunky or puréed with a handheld blender.

basic béchamel sauce

This classic white sauce can be used as the base of a creamy vegetable sauce. It's also good in a chicken or vegetable pie filling with ingredients such as spinach, mushrooms, ham, or seafood. For a cheese-style sauce, stir in 4 ounces shredded sharp cheddar cheese after the sauce has thickened.

To serve 4 (makes 1 1/2 cups)	To make in bulk (6 cups)	
2 tbsp.	1/2 cup	butter or margarine
3 tbsp.	3/4 cup	all-purpose flour
1 1/2 cups	6 cups	milk
pinch	1/2 tsp.	ground nutmeg
		sea salt and white pepper

Melt the butter or margarine in a saucepan, then stir in the flour and cook over low heat for 2 minutes, stirring constantly. Slowly add the milk, then increase the heat slightly and bring to a boil, stirring until the sauce thickens. Add the nutmeg and season with salt and pepper to taste.

For a dairy-free version, use soy margarine or 2 tablespoons sunflower or olive oil, and use soy milk in place of cow's milk. For a reduced-fat version, use 2 tablespoons sunflower or olive oil, and 2 percent or 1 percent milk.

chicken stock

Make chicken stock from a chicken carcass and fresh vegetables as well as with vegetable scraps and peelings, avoiding root ends, dirty scrapings, and starchy vegetables such as potatoes. Ensure a good mix of vegetables to avoid having a dominant flavor. This stock freezes well.

1 chicken carcass, including the skin
1 large onion, roughly chopped
1 carrot, scrubbed and roughly chopped
1 celery stick, roughly chopped
vegetable peelings (see note above)
1 garlic clove, chopped
2 bay leaves
1 bunch fresh parsley
1/2 tsp. salt
1/2 tsp. whole peppercorns
water

Put the all the ingredients in a large saucepan and cover with water. Bring to a boil over high heat. Reduce the heat and simmer, uncovered, for at least 1 hour, preferably 2 or 3. Cool, skim off any visible fat, and strain. Use within 5 days or freeze.

To save on freezer space, reduce the stock by half by boiling vigorously. Cool and pour into ice cube trays. When frozen, put the cubes into a resealable plastic bag. Then, when needed, simply pop a cube in a mug and add boiling water to dissolve the cube. Alternately, freeze in small plastic boxes.

Makes approximately 4 cups

starters

A good appetizer should wake up the taste buds and whet the appetite for the meal to come. It should be full of bright flavors and look delectable. The following starters are perfect. Many combine sweet and sour notes or have soft and crunchy textures — with a bit of affordable luxury, to boot.

feta figs with parma ham

see variations page 32

The ultimate quick-fix starter designed to impress. For the best results, be sure that figs are in season, when they are ripe and tasty. If you are disappointed in your figs, don't despair; make the baked fig variation on page 32.

3 tbsp. olive oil
1 tbsp. balsamic vinegar
salt and pepper
8 ripe figs, halved

4 oz. crumbled feta cheese
8 slices Parma ham or other dry-cured ham
handful of watercress or salad leaves
1 tsp. fresh mint, chopped

Whisk together the oil and vinegar and a pinch each of salt and pepper until well blended.

Arrange the figs, feta cheese, ham, and watercress or salad leaves on individual serving plates. Sprinkle with the mint and drizzle over the salad dressing just before serving.

Serves 4

hot camembert with cranberry sauce

see variations page 33

Break the ice with this great dish to share. It looks impressive, but is so easy to make.

1 whole Camembert wheel (preferably in a
    wooden box)
2 tbsp. olive oil
salt and black pepper

French bread or Italian breadsticks, to serve

for the sauce
12 oz. cranberries
1 cup brown sugar
grated zest of 1 orange
1/2 cup orange juice
2 tbsp. port (optional)

Unwrap the Camembert, then put it back in the wooden box and place on a heatproof plate; if there is no box, place on a sheet of baking parchment in a small heatproof dish. Drizzle with olive oil and a grind of salt and black pepper. Bake at 400°F for 12–15 minutes, until it is oozing when touched and brown on the top.

Meanwhile, combine all the ingredients for the sauce in a saucepan and simmer for 10 minutes, stirring occasionally. Set aside and allow to cool slightly; it should be served warm, but not scalding. Place in four individual serving dishes.

Serve the Camembert in the box, like a fondue, using the French bread or breadsticks as dippers, accompanied by the cranberry sauce.

Serves 4

bruschetta with ham & artichokes

see variations page 34

An elegant bruschetta that is full of classic Italian flavors. You can also make in bulk as a canapé.

8 slices French bread or ciabatta
1 garlic clove, halved
8 tsp. olive oil
8 thin slices of smoked ham or Parma ham

8 oz. marinated or charbroiled artichokes from a jar, drained
4 tbsp. Parmesan shavings
1 tsp. fresh basil leaves, torn

Rub one side of each slice of bread with the cut side of the garlic clove. Drizzle each with a teaspoon of olive oil. Put the bread under the broiler and toast lightly on both sides.

Lay 1 ham slice onto each piece of toasted bread. Chop larger pieces of artichoke into bite-size pieces, then pile on top of the ham. Finish with Parmesan shavings and basil leaves.

Serves 4

southern spiced nuts

see variations page 35

A spicy appetizer that is perfect for an informal start to the evening. Packed into a jar, these nuts make great hostess gifts too.

2 tbsp. butter
1 cup pecan halves
1 cup dry-roasted unsalted peanuts
1 cup whole almonds
1 tbsp. Worcestershire sauce

1 tsp. chili powder
1/4 tsp. cumin powder
1/4 tsp. salt
1/4 tsp. black pepper

Preheat the oven to 350°F. Put the butter in a foil-lined shallow baking pan large enough to hold the nuts in a single layer. Put pan in the oven to melt the butter. Add the nuts and Worcestershire sauce, and toss to coat the nuts evenly in the mixture. Combine the chili powder, cumin powder, salt, and pepper and sprinkle evenly over the nuts, then toss to coat. Bake the nuts until toasted, 15–20 minutes, stirring after 10 minutes.

Remove the nuts from the oven. Put in a bowl and serve immediately. Can be made the day before, in which case cool the nuts completely, then keep in an airtight container until ready to serve.

Makes 3 cups; serves 6–8

blinis with salmon, capers & herbed cheese

see variations page 36

These delicious starters can be made in minutes using store-bought blinis.

1/2 cup ricotta or cream cheese
1 tbsp. fresh chopped dill
1/2 tbsp. caper berries
salt and black pepper

8 blinis
1/2 cup (about 2 slices) smoked salmon pieces
2 thin slices of lemon, quartered, to garnish

Combine the cheese, dill, and caper berries with salt and pepper to taste. Spread on the blinis. Top with smoked salmon, garnished with a quarter of a slice of lemon.

Serves 4

shrimp with watercress dip

see variations page 37

A simple yet yummy starter. Be sure to get the freshest and best shrimp possible for this dish. Serve with elegant triangles of lightly buttered whole-wheat bread.

16–24 cooked shrimp in their shells, depending
   on their size
1 bunch watercress

2/3 cup sour cream
grated zest of 1 lemon
salt and pepper

Wash the shrimp, dry thoroughly, then arrange around the edge of a serving plate.

Take half of the watercress and chop finely in a food processor, or by hand with a sharp knife. Stir into the sour cream. Add the lemon zest with salt and pepper to taste. Transfer the dip to a bowl and place in the center of the serving plate; arrange the remaining watercress to surround the bowl.

Serves 4

anchovy deviled eggs

see variations page 38

This old-fashioned appetizer is always welcome and works well as a starter, with cocktails, or at a buffet. It has limitless variations, so use those suggested here as a springboard for your own ideas. The flavored yolk can simply be spooned back into the egg white or, if you want to impress, use a piping bag and form the yolk into rosettes.

4 large eggs, at room temperature
1 tbsp. vinegar
4 tbsp. mayonnaise or plain yogurt
2 tsp. minced anchovy fillets

1 tsp. lemon juice
salt and paprika
4 anchovy fillets, halved, to garnish
tiny sprigs of fresh parsley, to garnish

Put the eggs in a saucepan large enough to hold them snugly in one layer. Cover with sufficient water to cover them by at least 1 inch and add the vinegar. Gently bring to a boil and simmer for 7 minutes. Use a timer; do not overcook or the yolks will develop a black ring. Remove the eggs from the pan and cool under cold running water for 1 minute. Set aside until cool enough to peel — they peel more easily when warm. Tap the shells all over, then remove them. Rinse under cold water to remove any bits of shell.

When the eggs are cool, slice lengthwise and scoop out the yolk. Press yolks through a sieve or mash in a bowl. Beat in the mayonnaise or yogurt, minced anchovy, and lemon juice, then season with salt and paprika to taste.

Spoon or pipe the egg yolk back into the whites, and garnish each egg half with half an anchovy fillet and a parsley sprig.

Serves 4

oven-baked onion bhajis with mint raita

see variations page 39

These Indian appetizers are traditionally made by deep frying, which, although delicious, makes them high in fat. Oven-baked bhajis offer a healthier alternative, but if you want to be authentic, deep-fry in hot oil (375°F) for 8 minutes, turning once. Although bhajis are usually made with gram flour made from ground garbanzo beans, all-purpose flour can use substituted.

for the bhajis
- 1 large onion
- 1 tbsp. sunflower oil
- 1/2 tsp. turmeric
- 1 cup gram (garbanzo) flour or all-purpose flour
- 1 tsp. garam masala spice mix
- 1 tbsp. mango chutney
- 1 tbsp. lemon juice
- pinch chili powder
- generous pinch salt
- water

for the mint raita
- 1/2 cup plain yogurt
- 1 tbsp. mint sauce from a jar
- 1/2 tsp. turmeric

Preheat oven to 350°F. Line a cookie sheet with baking parchment. Cut the onions in half, then slice width-wise. Heat the oil in a skillet, and fry the onion and turmeric for 5–7 minutes until softened, stirring occasionally.

Meanwhile, mix all the other bhaji ingredients in a bowl, adding a little water to form a very thick batter. Stir in the fried onion and form into 8 small balls, flattening each one slightly on the cookie sheet. Bake for about 15 minutes or until crisp.

While the bhajis are cooking, make the mint sauce by combining all the ingredients together in a small bowl.

Serves 4

feta figs with parma ham

see base recipe page 19

stilton pears with parma ham
Peel, halve, and core 4 ripe pears; rub the flesh gently with lemon juice to prevent discoloration. Prepare the basic recipe, replacing figs and feta cheese with pears and Stilton. Replace olive oil with walnut oil, if desired.

cantaloupe with parmesan & parma ham
Peel a cantaloupe and remove the seeds. Cut into bite-size pieces. Prepare the basic recipe, replacing figs and feta cheese with cantaloupe pieces and 2 ounces Parmesan shavings.

baked feta figs with parma ham
Arrange the figs in a baking dish and sprinkle with a little sugar. Bake at 400°F for about 15 minutes, until the tops of the figs are just beginning to caramelize. Sprinkle feta over the top and return to the oven just to warm, 2–3 minutes. Proceed as for basic recipe.

feta figs with walnuts
Prepare the basic recipe, replacing ham with 2/3 cup walnut halves. Toast the walnuts in a heavy skillet over high heat for about 3 minutes, stirring frequently, until just browned. Remove from the pan and let cool before using to complete the basic recipe.

hot camembert with cranberry sauce

see base recipe page 21

baked brie with cranberry sauce
Prepare the basic recipe, replacing the camembert with a miniature brie.

baked camembert with caramelized onions
Prepare the basic recipe, replacing the cranberry sauce with a jar of
caramelized onion conserve.

baked camembert with rhubarb sauce
Prepare the basic recipe, replacing cranberries with prepared rhubarb, cut into
1-inch pieces.

baked camembert fondue with crudites
Prepare the basic recipe, omitting the cranberry sauce. Serve with fruit crudites
such as apple and pear wedges (dipped in lemon juice to prevent discoloration),
black and green grapes, toasted pecans or walnuts, and breadsticks.

bruschetta with ham & artichokes

see base recipe page 22

bruschetta with white bean purée
Prepare the basic recipe but omit topping. Mash (or blend in food processor) 1 cup canned cannellini beans, drained, with 2 tablespoons olive oil, 1 tablespoon lemon juice, 1 tablespoon chopped fresh parsley, 1 small crushed garlic clove, and salt and pepper to taste. Spread on top of the toasted bread and serve garnished with paprika.

bruschetta with grilled peppers
Prepare the basic recipe, replacing the artichokes with jarred grilled peppers.

bruschetta with pâté
Prepare the basic recipe, replacing ham with a good-quality pâté. Top with artichokes or grilled peppers. Omit Parmesan shavings and basil.

bruschetta with tomatoes & herbs
Prepare the basic recipe but omit topping. Chop 3 medium vine-ripened tomatoes and mix with 2 tablespoons chopped sundried tomatoes in oil, 3 tablespoons torn basil leaves, 2 tablespoons finely chopped red onion, 2 tablespoons olive oil, 1 teaspoon lemon juice, 1/4 teaspoon sugar, and freshly ground salt and black pepper. Can be served cold or warmed under a low broiler for 5 minutes.

variations

southern spiced nuts

see base recipe page 24

indian spiced nuts
Prepare the basic recipe, replacing butter with peanut or hazelnut oil and omitting Worcestershire sauce. Replace the seasonings with 1 teaspoon ground cumin, 1 teaspoon ground coriander, 1 teaspoon garam masala spice mix, 1/2 teaspoon cayenne pepper, and 1/2 teaspoon turmeric. Add 1/2 cup raisins or coconut, if desired.

christmas spiced nuts
Prepare the basic recipe, omitting Worcestershire sauce and replacing the seasonings with 1/2 cup sugar, 1 teaspoon ground cinnamon, 1 teaspoon ground ginger, and 1/8 teaspoon ground nutmeg, with cayenne pepper and salt to taste.

chili spiced peanuts
Prepare basic recipe, replacing mixed nuts with 3 cups unsalted dry-roasted peanuts, and seasoning with 1 tablespoon chili powder and 1 teaspoon cumin.

variations

blinis with salmon, capers & herbed cheese

see base recipe page 25

blinis with smoked ham & herbed cheese

Prepare the basic recipe, replacing the dill with 1/2 tablespoon chopped parsley and 1/2 teaspoon chopped chives, and replacing the smoked salmon with smoked ham. Garnish with quarter of a cherry tomato.

blinis with cheese, dill & cucumber

Prepare the basic recipe, omitting caper berries. Replace salmon with cucumber slices. Drizzle with lemon juice. Garnish with fresh dill.

blinis with herbed cheese & sundried tomatoes

Prepare the basic recipe, replacing the dill with basil. Replace salmon with 4 sundried tomato halves, chopped into pieces. Garnish with half a black olive.

blinis with spicy herbed cheese & shrimp

Prepare the basic recipe, omitting caper berries. Replace dill with cilantro and add 1/4–1/2 teaspoon chopped red chile to the cheese. Replace salmon with 2 small shrimp or 1 large shrimp per blini. Replace lemon garnish with lime.

shrimp with watercress dip

see base recipe page 26

vegetable crudites with watercress dip
Prepare the watercress dip as directed. Serve surrounded by vegetable sticks —
cucumber, celery, carrot — plus small whole vegetables such as snow peas and
baby corn. Accompany with breadsticks and chips.

shrimp with mediterranean dip
Replace the watercress dip by combining 1/4 cup sour cream, 3/4 cup hummus,
1/2 cup crumbled feta cheese, 1/4 cup green onion, 1/4 cup very finely
chopped red bell pepper, 1 crushed garlic clove, 1/4 teaspoon cumin, and salt
and pepper to taste.

shrimp with spicy dip
Replace the watercress dip by combining 1 cup mayonnaise and 2–4 teaspoons
harissa paste to taste (add a little at a time). Flavor with 1 teaspoon lime juice,
1 teaspoon honey, and 1 tablespoon freshly chopped cilantro.

shrimp with russian sauce
Replace the watercress dip by combining 1 cup mayonnaise, 1/4 cup ketchup,
1 tablespoon Worcestershire sauce or horseradish, 2 tablespoons minced onion,
and 1 tablespoon each of finely chopped red and green bell pepper.

variations

anchovy deviled eggs

see base recipe page 29

simple deviled eggs
Prepare the basic recipe, omitting the anchovy and lemon juice and flavoring the mashed egg yolk with 1 teaspoon prepared mustard and 1 teaspoon vinegar. Garnish with chopped fresh parsley.

crabmeat eggs
Prepare the basic recipe, omitting the anchovy and flavoring the mashed egg yolk with 1/4 cup finely chopped crabmeat. Garnish with a tiny shrimp or a few flakes of crabmeat.

chili eggs
Prepare the basic recipe, omitting the anchovy and flavoring the mashed egg yolk with 2 tablespoons cream cheese, 1 teaspoon butter, 1/2 teaspoon chopped red chile or 1/4 teaspoon dried chili powder, and a pinch each of cumin and turmeric. Garnish with chopped cilantro.

blue cheese eggs
Prepare the basic recipe, omitting the anchovy and lemon juice and flavoring the mashed egg yolk with 4 tablespoons crumbled blue cheese, 2 tablespoons heavy cream or sour cream, and a pinch of cayenne pepper.

oven-baked onion bhajis with mint raita

see base recipe page 30

mixed vegetable bhajis
Prepare the basic recipe, replacing the onion with 1 1/2 cups frozen mixed vegetables, thawed.

onion bhajis with tomato chutney
Prepare the basic recipe, replacing mint raita with tomato chutney: grate 1-inch piece of fresh ginger. Heat 1 tablespoon oil in a pan; add ginger and 1 teaspoon crushed red pepper. Cook for 1 minute, then add 1 cup canned chopped tomatoes, 1/4 cup sugar, 1 tablespoon vinegar, and 1 tablespoon raisins. Stir while over medium heat until mixture thickens.

parsnip & black mustard seed pakora
Spread 1 1/2 cups shredded parsnip and 1 small minced garlic clove on a parchment-lined cookie sheet. Bake at 350°F for 10 minutes. Meanwhile, toast 1 tablespoon black mustard seed in a dry pan until it pops. Prepare the basic recipe, replacing the onion with the parsnip and black mustard seed.

onion bhaji wraps
Prepare the basic recipe. Take 4 wraps and spread with a little mango chutney. Add shredded lettuce, then top with 2 warm prepared onion bhajis that have each been cut in half. Spoon mint raita on top. Roll and serve hot or cold.

soups

Home-cooked soups are probably the easiest of
dishes to make — and one of the most satisfying.
It's homey food, so chop away, no need to worry
about precision — but remember, the smaller the
pieces, the quicker the cooking time. Soup needs
bread, and there is a fabulous choice of artisan
breads available. Look for them in the store or the
farmers' market and freeze until required.

tomato pesto soup

see variations page 54

Everyone loves tomato soup, and this one is richly flavored with pesto. Serve with artisan bread and sheep cheese such as Manchego for a wholesome feast.

2 tbsp. olive oil
2 garlic cloves, halved
3 (14-oz.) cans tomatoes
1 small potato, peeled and chopped
2 cups chicken broth or vegetable bouillon

1 tsp. sugar
salt and pepper
1/2 cup pesto from a jar
1/3 cup sour cream, to serve

Heat the olive oil in a large saucepan and add the garlic, cook for 3 minutes to soften and brown, then remove from the oil and discard. Add the canned tomatoes and cook for 5 minutes over medium heat, stirring occasionally. Add the potato, broth, and sugar; season with salt and pepper to taste. Bring to a boil, reduce the heat, and simmer for 10 minutes.

Purée the soup using a stick blender. Stir in half of the pesto and adjust seasoning to taste. Serve using the remaining pesto and the sour cream to swirl into the soup as it is served.

Serves 6

clam & corn chowder

see variations page 55

This classic is a substantial soup that is a meal in itself. Clam juice is used in this version for a deliciously rich, fishy taste; if you prefer something milder, use vegetable bouillon instead.

2 tbsp. butter or oil
3 strips of bacon, chopped
1 large onion, chopped
2 celery ribs, chopped
3 medium potatoes, diced
2 tbsp. all-purpose flour
1 (8-oz.) bottle clam juice
1 bay leaf

1/2 tsp. salt
1/4 tsp. black pepper
2 cups milk or half and half
2 (7-oz.) cans minced or whole clams, drained
1 (7-oz.) can corn or 1 cup frozen corn
fresh parsley, to garnish
crackers, to serve

Melt the butter (or heat the oil) in a saucepan and add the bacon. Fry for a few minutes, stirring until crisp. Add the onion and celery and cook for another 5 minutes, until the onion is soft. Add the potatoes and stir until coated with fat, then sift in the flour and stir to distribute. Add the clam juice, bay leaf, salt, and pepper. Bring to a boil, stirring, then simmer for about 10 minutes, until the potatoes are cooked but holding their shape.

Add the milk or half and half, clams, and corn to the chowder. Warm through without boiling (which may cause curdling) and adjust the seasoning to taste. Remove the bay leaf. Serve garnished with chopped parsley, accompanied by crackers.

Serves 4

carrot & cilantro soup

see variations page 56

This soup is bright and cheerful in appearance and taste. It makes a good starter or light meal, and is super healthy served with some chunky whole-grain bread.

2 tbsp. sunflower oil
1 medium onion, chopped
1 tsp. ground coriander
1 medium potato, washed or peeled
1 1/4 lb. carrots, washed or peeled
5 cups chicken broth or vegetable bouillon

1 bay leaf
salt and pepper
2 tbsp. chopped fresh cilantro, plus more
    to garnish
half and half or soy creamer, optional

Heat the oil in a saucepan, then add the onion. Cook gently for about 5 minutes until softened, stirring occasionally. Add the ground coriander and cook for 1 additional minute.

While the onions are cooking, finely chop the potatoes and carrots in a food processor or by hand. Add to the onions and coriander, and cook for 2 minutes, stirring. Add the broth or bouillon and bay leaf, and bring to a boil. Cover and simmer over low heat for 10 minutes or until the potatoes and carrots are soft. Stir in the cilantro and, using a stick blender or food processor, purée until smooth. Season to taste with salt and pepper. Reheat, if necessary, and serve with a drizzle of half and half or soy creamer, garnished with a sprig of cilantro.

Serves 4–6

thai coconut chicken soup

see variations page 57

This may not be an authentic recipe, but it closely resembles its Thai cousin without all the hard-to-find ingredients.

2 tbsp. sunflower oil
12 oz. boneless chicken meat, thinly sliced
2 (14-oz.) cans coconut milk
2 cups chicken broth
6 shiitake or cremini mushrooms, sliced
2 tbsp. fresh ginger, minced
1 tsp. lemongrass paste

4 tbsp. fish sauce
1/3 cup lime juice
1/4 tsp. cayenne pepper
1/2 tsp. brown sugar
5 green onions, chopped
1/2 cup grape tomatoes, halved
1/4 cup chopped fresh cilantro

Heat the oil in a large saucepan and flash-fry the chicken until it turns white, 2–3 minutes. Add the coconut milk and broth, and bring to a boil. Reduce the heat. Add the mushrooms, ginger, lemongrass paste, fish sauce, lime juice, cayenne, and sugar, and simmer for 10 minutes, or until the chicken is cooked through. Sprinkle the green onions, tomatoes, and cilantro on top, and serve while hot.

Serves 6

leek & lentil soup

see variations page 58

A soul-warming soup for a winter day. Using canned lentils cuts down the cooking time. Dried green lentils can be substituted, but they take 30–40 minutes to cook. Use good-quality broth or bouillon.

1 tbsp. butter
2 medium leeks, finely sliced
2 garlic cloves, minced
1 tsp. paprika
1/2 tsp. ground cumin

1 (15-oz.) can green lentils, drained, or
   1 1/2 cups cooked lentils
4 cups chicken broth or vegetable bouillon
salt and pepper
4 tbsp. yogurt
1/4 cup fresh chopped parsley

Melt the butter in a saucepan and add the leeks and garlic. Sauté for 5 minutes, stirring frequently, until the leeks are soft and clear. Stir in the paprika and cumin, and cook for 1 minute. Add the lentils and broth with salt and pepper to taste. Bring to a boil, then reduce the heat and simmer for 10 minutes. Use a stick blender to partially blend the soup, leaving plenty of texture, or remove 1 pint of soup and blend in the food processor, return to the pan, and reheat the soup, if necessary. Serve garnished with the yogurt and parsley.

Serves 4

chicken tortilla soup

see variations page 59

This soup is full of the vibrant tastes associated with Mexican food. As in many traditional soups, bread — in the form of tortilla — is used to soak up the flavors and give extra body to the soup. Since the broth is exposed in this dish, choose the best available.

2 tbsp. corn or sunflower oil
1 medium red onion, chopped
1 red bell pepper, chopped
1 green bell pepper, chopped
1 jalapeño pepper, chopped
2 garlic cloves, minced
1 tsp. ground cumin
1/2–1 tsp. chili powder, to taste
1/2 tsp. ground coriander
2 tsp. dried oregano

1 cup canned chopped tomatoes
5 cups chicken broth or bouillon
12 oz. cooked chicken, shredded
2 cups canned or frozen corn
1/4 cup chopped fresh cilantro
juice of 1/2 lime
salt
tortilla chips, to serve and to garnish
avocado slices, to garnish

Heat the oil in a saucepan and add the onion, peppers, and garlic. Sauté for 5 minutes, stirring frequently. Add the cumin, chili powder, coriander, and oregano, and cook for 1 more minute. Add the tomatoes and broth or bouillon, bring to a boil, then reduce the heat and simmer for 10 minutes. Add the chicken and corn, and simmer for 5 minutes.

Remove the pan from the heat, stir in the cilantro and lime, and add salt to taste. Put a handful of tortilla chips in the bottom of each serving bowl and pour the soup on top. Serve garnished with a couple of tortilla chips and avocado slices.

Serves 4–6

shrimp bisque

see variations page 60

This is a rich, smooth soup based on the classic French recipe. It is perfect served with warm French bread and a glass of chilled Chablis.

2 tbsp. butter or margarine
5 green onions, sliced
1 garlic clove, minced
3 tbsp. all-purpose flour
2 pints fish bouillon or bottled clam juice
1 (15-oz.) can tomatoes
2/3 cup white wine or dry sherry
juice of 1/2 lemon

1 tbsp. Worcestershire sauce
1 tbsp. tomato paste
12 oz. cooked peeled shrimp
2/3 cup heavy cream
salt and pepper
1 tbsp. chopped fresh tarragon or parsley
lemon wedges, to garnish

Melt the butter or margarine in a saucepan and add the green onions and garlic. Cook, stirring frequently for 2 minutes, until soft. Stir in the flour and cook for 2 more minutes. Remove the pan from the heat and slowly incorporate the bouillon or clam juice, stirring to keep the soup smooth. Return to the heat and bring to a boil, stirring until thickened.

Add the tomatoes, wine or sherry (if using), lemon juice, Worcestershire sauce, and tomato paste, and cook for 5 minutes. Add the shrimp, then purée the soup using a stick blender or food processor. Stir in the cream, add salt and pepper to taste, then return to the heat for a couple of minutes to heat through without boiling. Serve garnished with tarragon or parsley and accompanied with a lemon wedge.

Serves 6

pea & mint soup

see variations page 61

This soup sings out with the flavors of summer, but since it is made with frozen peas, it can be enjoyed year round. It will become a family favorite — and one that you can make when you think you have nothing to eat.

2 tbsp. butter
1 medium sweet white or red onion, chopped
1 garlic clove
1 lb. bag frozen peas
1/2 cup fresh mint leaves, roughly chopped, or
    2 tsp. dried mint

2 cups vegetable bouillon
salt and pepper
1/4 cup half and half (optional)
crumbled bacon, to garnish (optional)

Melt the butter in a saucepan and add the onion and garlic. Sauté for 5 minutes, stirring frequently, until the onions are soft and clear. Stir in the peas, mint, bouillon, and salt and pepper to taste. Bring to a boil, then cover and simmer for 10 minutes.

Purée the soup using a stick blender, or in batches in a food processor. Stir in the half and half, if using, and return to the heat for a couple of minutes to heat through without boiling. Serve garnished with crumbled bacon, if desired.

Serves 4

variations

tomato pesto soup

see base recipe page 41

roasted red pepper soup
Prepare the basic recipe, replacing the pesto in the soup with 1 (12-ounce) jar of roasted bell peppers. Serve garnished with sour cream.

tomato orange soup
Prepare the basic recipe, replacing the pesto in the soup with the juice and rind of 1 orange and a bay leaf. Remove the bay leaf before blending. Serve garnished with sour cream or a drizzle of extra-virgin olive oil.

fresh tomato pesto soup
Prepare the basic recipe, replacing the canned tomatoes with 4 cups of chopped fresh tomatoes. The skins will be blended into the soup, but for an extra-fine texture, remove the skins before chopping. Extend the initial cooking time for fresh tomatoes to 10 minutes, stirring frequently to concentrate the flavor.

creamy tomato pesto soup
Prepare the basic recipe, increasing the quantity of sour cream to 2/3 cup. Add 1/3 cup of sour cream to the soup when blending.

clam & corn chowder

see base recipe page 43

corn & bean chowder
Prepare the basic recipe, using the vegetable bouillon liquid option and replacing the clams with 1 (15-ounce) can kidney beans. Add 1 tablespoon Worcestershire sauce to the chowder with the milk. For a vegetarian chowder, omit the bacon or replace with vegetarian bacon strips.

sardine & corn chowder
Prepare the basic recipe, replacing the clams with 2 (4-ounce) cans sardines packed in water or oil, drained well and lightly crushed.

spicy sausage & corn chowder
Take 12 ounces spicy Italian sausage or chorizo, remove casings, and break into small pieces. Fry with the bacon, drain off most of the fat, and continue with basic recipe, replacing clam juice with chicken or vegetable broth and omitting the clams. Garnish with cilantro.

turkey & corn chowder
Prepare the basic recipe, replacing clam juice with turkey or chicken broth. Replace clams with 2 cups cooked turkey pieces. If using up festive leftovers, other vegetables such as carrots, peas, and mushrooms may be added, too.

variations

carrot & cilantro soup

see base recipe page 44

root vegetable & cilantro soup
Prepare the basic recipe, but instead of using carrots alone, use a combination of carrots, rutabaga, and parsnip.

butternut & cilantro soup
Prepare the basic recipe, replacing carrots with 1 pound butternut squash flesh.

carrot & cream cheese soup
Prepare the basic recipe, but stir 2 ounces cream cheese into the soup before serving. For an herby flavor, omit the ground coriander and the cilantro and use 2 ounces Boursin cheese. Omit the half and half garnish.

carrot & ginger soup
Prepare the basic recipe, replacing the ground coriander with 1 1/2 tablespoons of minced fresh ginger and 1/2 teaspoon ground cumin. Omit the cilantro. Serve garnished with yogurt and chopped parsley.

variations

thai coconut chicken soup

see base recipe page 47

thai coconut shrimp soup
Prepare the basic recipe, replacing the chicken with 12 ounces small raw shrimp. If using cooked shrimp, add with the mushrooms.

thai coconut, chicken & spinach soup
Prepare the basic recipe, adding 4 ounces spinach to the soup after it has simmered for 5 minutes. Continue to simmer for 5 more minutes, stirring to separate the spinach leaves.

hot coconut & chicken soup
Prepare the basic recipe, adding 1–2 red chiles, finely sliced, or 1/2–3/4 teaspoons dried crushed chile with the other ingredients.

thai coconut tofu soup
Prepare the basic recipe (or the spinach or hot variations above), omitting the chicken and replacing the chicken broth with a good vegetable bouillon. Add 1 (12-ounce) package silken tofu, diced, after the soup is cooked and heat through for 2 minutes.

variations

leek & lentil soup

see base recipe page 48

tomato & lentil soup
Prepare the basic recipe, but add 1 (15-ounce) can chopped tomato and
1 tablespoon tomato paste with the broth.

chicken & lentil soup
Prepare the basic recipe, adding 12 ounces shredded cooked chicken after
blending. Return to the heat for a few minutes to heat through.

egyptian lentil soup
Prepare the basic recipe, replacing leeks with 1 large onion. Increase the
cumin to 2 teaspoons, and add 1 teaspoon ground coriander and
1/2 teaspoon turmeric with the paprika. Squeeze the juice of 1/2 lemon into
the soup with the parsley. The yogurt is optional.

curried lentil soup
Prepare the basic recipe, but add 1 medium-size finely chopped potato and
1 small finely chopped carrot with the leek. Replace the cumin and paprika
with 2 tablespoons medium curry powder and 1/4 teaspoon cayenne pepper.
Add the juice of 1/2 lemon into the soup with the parsley.

chicken tortilla soup

see base recipe page 49

spicy chicken orzo soup
Prepare the basic recipe, but add 1/2 cup orzo (or other small pasta) with the broth. Replace the cilantro and lime with 2 tablespoons freshly chopped basil and 1 teaspoon lemon juice. Omit the tortillas and avocado.

black bean & tortilla soup
Prepare the basic recipe, replacing the shredded chicken with 1 (15-ounce) can of black beans, drained and rinsed. Replace the chicken broth with vegetable bouillon.

spicy chicken & lime rice soup
Prepare the basic recipe, but add 1/2 cup long grain rice with the broth and omit the tortilla and avocado. Serve with a wedge of lime.

mexican bread soup
Prepare the basic recipe, omitting the tortilla and avocado. Fry eight 1-inch slices of French bread or 2 sliced bolillos (crusty oval rolls) in oil until golden on both sides. Place in the bottom of a large soup tureen or bowl. Top with 1/2 cup each of raisins and sliced green olives, 4 sliced pitted prunes, and 2 hard-boiled eggs. Pour the hot soup over and serve immediately.

variations

shrimp bisque

see base recipe page 50

crab or lobster bisque
Prepare the basic recipe, replacing the shrimp with 12 ounces fresh or canned crabmeat or lobster meat.

chicken bisque
Prepare the basic recipe, replacing fish bouillon with chicken broth and omitting shrimp and lemon wedges. Once the soup is blended, add 12 ounces of shredded chicken with the cream.

cajun shrimp bisque
Prepare the basic recipe, adding 1–2 teaspoons of Cajun spices with the green onion.

tomato bisque
Prepare the basic recipe, replacing the fish bouillon with chicken broth or vegetable bouillon. Increase the tomato paste to 1/4 cup.

variations

pea & mint soup

see base recipe page 53

pea & ham soup
Prepare the basic recipe, replacing the mint with 1 teaspoon dried thyme. Once the soup is blended, stir in 8 ounces diced ham with the cream.

indian green pea soup
Prepare the basic recipe, omitting the cream and bacon. Add 2 tablespoons minced fresh ginger, 1–2 serrano chiles, 1/4 teaspoon ground cumin, and a bay leaf with the onion. Remove the bay leaf and chiles before blending, and add 1 tablespoon of lemon juice.

pea, zucchini & pesto soup
Prepare the basic recipe. After the onion has softened, add a large, sliced zucchini and cook until softened. Replace the mint leaves with 2 tablespoons of pesto.

french pea & lettuce soup
Prepare the basic recipe, but use 1 1/2 cups vegetable bouillon and 1/2 cup milk. After the peas have cooked, add a head of romaine lettuce, roughly chopped, and cook for a couple of minutes to wilt. This is best with the addition of half and half, although yogurt may be used instead.

salads

Salads are so quick to prepare and so versatile —
they make great meals in themselves, can double as
starters, and are ideal for cookouts and buffet-style
meals. This chapter contains a selection that will be
perfect for all occasions.

Don't feel bound by salad recipes. If you don't
have the exact ingredients, just use a different fruit
or vegetable, choosing something similar in
sweetness, texture, or flavor.

festive quinoa salad

see variations page 76

Quinoa is a wonder food — a grain native to South America that has become popular not only for its nutty flavor and crisp texture, but because it is rich in complete protein. This salad is terrific for a buffet family meal, or you can bulk up the recipe and take it to a potluck supper.

6 cups water
pinch salt
1 cup quinoa
4 green onions, sliced
1/2 cup sliced almonds or pistachios

4 tbsp. fresh chopped mint
seeds from 1 pomegranate
2 celery ribs, sliced
grated zest and juice of 1 lime
1/4 cup virgin olive oil or hazelnut oil

Bring the water and salt to a boil in a medium saucepan. Rinse the quinoa, then add to the pan, stirring and simmering until tender and the germ ring is visible, about 12 minutes. Drain, then cover with clean dishtowel and let sit for 5 minutes. Spread quinoa evenly onto cookie sheet and put in a cold place for about 10 minutes to cool.

Toast the almonds or pistachios in a heavy skillet until golden. Add to the quinoa with the mint, pomegranate seeds, celery, and the zest of the lime. Pour in the lime juice and the oil, and stir to mix.

Serves 4–5

creamy curried chicken salad

see variations page 77

Use low-fat mayonnaise and nonfat yogurt to keep this salad healthy. It is great accompanied by a rice or couscous salad, and is delicious over a baked potato or sweet potato. It only improves by being left to marinate, so it's a great salad to prepare ahead or take to a party.

1 lb. shredded chicken
4 green onions, sliced
2 celery ribs, sliced
3 tbsp. finely chopped dried apricots
2 tbsp. slivered almonds, to garnish

for the dressing
1/2 cup mayonnaise
1/4 cup yogurt
1/2–1 1/2 tbsp. medium curry powder
1 tsp. Worcestershire sauce
2 tbsp. mango chutney
salt and pepper
1 tsp. lemon or lime juice
1/2 cup chopped fresh cilantro, divided
arugula leaves, to serve

Place the chicken, green onions, celery, and apricots in a bowl. Toast the almonds in a dry skillet, turning frequently until lightly golden. Set aside to cool.

For the dressing, combine all of the ingredients in a bowl, adjusting the quantities of spices, seasonings, and chutney to taste (different brands vary hugely in strength) and reserving about 2 tablespoons of the cilantro for garnish.

Toss the chicken mixture with the dressing and serve on a bed of arugula leaves, garnished with the reserved chopped cilantro and toasted almonds.
Serves 4

warm five-spice duck & mango salad

see variations page 78

This is a rich, substantial salad that makes an excellent supper dish or centerpiece of a summer lunch — simply serve with some good crusty bread. If entertaining, you can prepare the salad ahead and simply cook the duck just before serving.

for the salad
2 tbsp. honey
2 medium-size duck breasts
1 tsp. Chinese five-spice powder
1/4 tsp. salt
2 oz. thin green beans
2 oz. snow peas
2 oz. baby corn
6 oz. mixed green salad leaves
4 green onions, diagonally sliced
1 cup alfalfa sprouts
1 medium mango, peeled and sliced
1 tbsp. sesame seeds

for the dressing
1 tsp. honey
1 tbsp. hot water
1/4 cup sunflower oil
1 tbsp. sesame oil
1 tsp. minced fresh ginger
1 tbsp. lime juice or rice wine vinegar
1 tbsp. soy sauce
generous pinch black pepper

Preheat the broiler. Using a pastry brush, brush the honey all over the duck breasts, then sprinkle with the Chinese five-spice powder and salt. Broil the duck breasts skin side up for 10 minutes, taking care as the hot fat can spit. Turn over and broil the flesh side for another 5 minutes. The duck should be still slightly pink inside. Let it rest for 5 minutes.

While the duck is cooking, blanch the green beans, snow peas, and baby corn in boiling water for 2 minutes. Drain, then rinse under cold water to refresh. Leave in cold water for a few minutes to cool.

For the dressing, dissolve the honey in the hot water in a clean jar, add all of the remaining dressing ingredients, and shake vigorously.

Combine the salad leaves, cooled and drained vegetables, alfalfa sprouts, and mango in a salad bowl. Thinly slice the duck breast and arrange on top of the salad. Pour the dressing over, garnish with sesame seeds, and serve immediately.

Serves 4

gorgonzola, spinach & pecan salad

see variations page 79

Such a classic! Serve as a starter for six or a family meal for four. If you like your pecans sweetened, add a couple of pinches of brown sugar just before the nuts have finished toasting — or try using the spiced nuts on page 24.

1 cup pecan halves
pinch salt
1 package baby spinach leaves
6 small vine-ripened tomatoes, quartered
1/2 small red onion, finely sliced
4 oz. Gorgonzola cheese, crumbled

for the dressing
1/4 cup olive oil
2 tbsp. red wine vinegar
pinch of salt and black pepper

Toast the pecans in a dry skillet for about 5 minutes, stirring frequently. Sprinkle with a pinch of salt. Remove to a plate and set aside to cool.

In a salad bowl, toss together the spinach, tomatoes, onion, and cheese. For the dressing, combine the ingredients by placing in a clean jar and shaking to mix. Add the pecans to the salad and toss with the dressing.

Serves 4

green bean, ham & quail egg salad

see variations page 80

Quail eggs are so creamy and delicious, but plain old eggs work almost as well in this tasty French-inspired salad. This is a particularly versatile dish that can be used on any occasion. If making ahead, cover and keep in the refrigerator until 30 minutes before serving; the flavors will be diminished if served too cold.

8 oz. fine green beans
12 quail eggs
4 slices Parma or other air-dried ham, torn into shreds
8 grape tomatoes, halved

for the dressing
1 garlic clove, minced
3 tbsp. olive oil
2 tbsp. crème fraîche or sour cream
1 tsp. teriyaki sauce
salt and pepper

Steam the green beans for 5–7 minutes until just cooked, but still with a bit of crunch. Rinse under cold water to refresh, then leave in cold water for a few minutes to cool. Simmer the quail eggs in boiling water for 2 1/2 minutes, then run under cold water to cool. Halve lengthwise.

For the dressing, mash the yolk of 1 quail egg in a bowl with the minced garlic. Gradually whisk in the olive oil, crème fraîche or sour cream, teriyaki sauce, and salt and pepper to taste.

In a shallow dish, arrange the green beans, ham, and tomatoes, then toss with the dressing. Add the eggs and toss once.

Serves 4

lentil & goat cheese salad

see variations page 81

This recipe uses canned lentils to make it an almost-instant fine and filling salad.
Nutritionally, it's a star. Simply serve with warm, crusty whole-wheat bread.

1 (15-oz.) can green lentils, drained, or
   1 1/2 cups cooked lentils
1 small red onion, sliced
1 medium red bell pepper, sliced
1 avocado, sliced and dipped in lemon juice
1 cup sliced cucumber

for the dressing
3 tbsp. olive oil
1 tbsp. balsamic vinegar
1 tsp. fresh chopped thyme or 1/4 tsp.
   dried thyme
large pinch salt
large pinch pepper
3 oz. goat cheese, crumbled
pea shoots or mixed salad lettuce leaves,
   to serve

Gently mix together the lentils, onion, pepper, avocado, and cucumber. For the dressing,
combine the ingredients by placing in a clean jar and shaking to mix. Carefully stir into the
salad. Arrange the salad on a bed of pea shoots or mixed salad leaves, and top with the
crumbled goat cheese.

Serves 4

mediterranean halloumi salad

see variations page 82

This salad is wonderful served with flatbread or pita. It hails from Cyprus, the home of halloumi cheese. This is a good salad for an outdoor party, particularly for vegetarians. Make the salad ahead of time, then grill the halloumi when you're ready to eat.

1/4 cup olive oil, plus extra to finish
1 medium red onion, sliced
2 garlic cloves, minced
2 red chiles, deseeded and chopped
pinch sugar
3 tbsp. white wine vinegar
2 (15-oz.) cans garbanzo beans
salt and black pepper

12 oz. tomatoes, chopped
1/4 cup sundried tomatoes, drained and
    chopped
1/2 cup fresh chopped parsley
1/4 cup fresh chopped mint
4 green onions, chopped
8 oz. halloumi cheese, sliced

Heat the olive oil in a skillet and cook the onion, garlic, chiles, and sugar over medium heat for 5 minutes until soft, then stir in the vinegar. Cook for 3 minutes until the vinegar has reduced by about half.

In a salad bowl, mix the onion mixture into the garbanzo beans. Season with plenty of salt and pepper. Toss in the tomatoes, sundried tomatoes, parsley, mint, and green onions. Drizzle extra olive oil over to moisten.

Place the halloumi slices under a preheated broiler or on the grill, and cook until golden brown on both sides, about 2 minutes per side. Serve on top of the salad.

Serves 4

german-style potato salad with sausage

see variations page 83

This version of potato salad uses a mustardy vinaigrette instead of mayonnaise for a lighter feel. It is essential to pour the dressing over hot potatoes, since they absorb the dressing as they cool.

2 lbs. small Yukon Gold or red potatoes, washed
    and halved
salt
1 tbsp. sunflower oil
8 oz. kielbasa or Polish sausage, sliced into
    1/4-inch-thick slices

for the dressing
1/3 cup olive oil
2 tbsp. white wine vinegar
2 tsp. grainy Dijon mustard
1 garlic clove, minced
salt and pepper
1/3 cup finely chopped chives or green onions
1/4 cup chopped flat-leaf parsley
2 tbsp. finely chopped tarragon or dill

Put the potatoes into a large saucepan. Add salt and enough water to cover generously. Bring the water to a boil over medium-high heat, then reduce the heat and simmer until potatoes are tender, about 15 minutes. Drain potatoes and set aside until cool enough to handle.

Meanwhile, in a skillet, heat the sunflower oil and brown the sausage. Drain on paper towels.

While the sausage and potatoes are cooking, prepare the dressing. In a clean jar, mix together the olive oil, vinegar, mustard, garlic, and salt and pepper to taste.

Cut the warm potatoes into 1/3-inch-thick slices and transfer to a large bowl with the sausage. (If you don't like potatoes with the skin on, peel them.) Add the chives or green onions, parsley, and tarragon or dill. Pour the dressing over and toss gently to coat. Serve at room temperature.

Serves 6–8

festive quinoa salad

see base recipe page 63

festive rice salad
Prepare the basic recipe, replacing the cooked quinoa and green onions with 3 cups cooked rice and finely sliced red onion.

festive tabbouleh
Prepare the basic recipe, replacing the cooked quinoa with 3 cups cooked couscous.

citrus & fennel quinoa salad
Prepare the basic recipe, replacing the pomegranate, mint, and celery with the chopped flesh of half a pink grapefruit and 1 orange, and 1 small fennel bulb, finely sliced.

summer quinoa salad
Prepare the basic recipe, omitting almonds and pomegranate. Chop the flesh of 1 avocado and put into the lime juice, then add to the cooled quinoa with 1/2 chopped red bell pepper, 8 halved grape tomatoes, 1/2 cup black olives, and 1/2 cup diced cucumber. Replace mint with cilantro, if desired.

variations

creamy curried chicken salad

see base recipe page 65

curried chicken wrap
Prepare the basic recipe. Spread 1/4 cup of curried chicken salad on a wrap.
Top with 1 teaspoon chopped cilantro, a few arugula leaves, and a sprinkling
of almonds.

chipotle chicken salad
Prepare the basic recipe, replacing the curry powder, Worcestershire sauce,
and mango chutney with 2 canned chipotle chiles, finely chopped, and
1 tablespoon adobo sauce.

curried salmon salad
Prepare the basic recipe, replacing the chicken with 4 cooked salmon fillets
(about 1 pound), skinned and roughly chopped. Replace the dried apricot
with dried or fresh mango.

variations

warm five-spice duck & mango salad

see base recipe page 66

warm chicken & mango salad
Prepare the basic recipe, replacing the duck with chicken breasts. Grill the chicken for 8–10 minutes on each side, ensuring that it is cooked through.

pulled pork & mango salad
Prepare the basic recipe for the salad and dressing. Replace the duck with 12 ounces pulled pork. Serve cold.

warm duck with spicy plum dressing
Prepare the basic recipe, using a dressing made from 1 tablespoon sunflower oil, 2 tablespoons each of plum sauce and Thai chili sauce, and 1 tablespoon water.

warm duck with asparagus & peach salad
Prepare the basic recipe, replacing the mango, snow peas, beans, and corn with 12 ounces cooked asparagus and the sliced flesh of 2 ripe peaches.

gorgonzola, spinach & pecan salad

see base recipe page 69

feta, spinach & pine nut salad
Prepare the basic recipe, replacing pecans and Gorgonzola with pine nuts and feta cheese.

goat cheese, spinach & walnut salad
Prepare the basic recipe, replacing pecans and Gorgonzola with walnuts and goat cheese.

wilted spinach, bacon & pecan salad
Prepare the basic recipe. Pan-fry 6 strips of bacon until crispy. Remove the bacon from the skillet, leaving the bacon grease. Drain on paper towels. When cool enough to handle, break into small pieces. Add the dressing ingredients to the skillet, reducing the olive oil to 2 tablespoons. Heat through (don't boil) and toss over the prepared salad with the bacon.

gorgonzola, spinach & apple salad
Prepare the basic recipe, omitting the pecans. Core and slice a crisp apple such as Granny Smith and dip in lemon juice to prevent discoloration. Toss into the salad.

green bean, ham & quail egg salad

see base recipe page 70

green bean, ham & egg salad
Prepare the basic recipe, replacing the 12 cooked quail eggs with 6 regular hard-boiled eggs.

green bean, sundried tomato & egg salad
Prepare the basic recipe, replacing ham with 1 cup sundried tomatoes in oil, drained and roughly chopped. Garnish with a few sliced black olives.

green bean, tuna & egg salad
Prepare the basic recipe, replacing the ham with 1 (6-ounce) can tuna, drained and flaked.

green bean, goat cheese & egg salad
Prepare the basic recipe, replacing the ham with 2 ounces crumbled goat cheese and garnishing with 1 tablespoon toasted pine nuts.

variations

lentil & goat cheese salad

see base recipe page 72

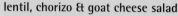

lentil, chorizo & goat cheese salad
Prepare the basic recipe, omitting the avocado and cucumber. In a skillet, gently fry 3 ounces chorizo slices for 3 minutes, then add the onion, red pepper, and 1 sliced green pepper. Cook for 5 minutes, until just soft. Drain on paper towels to remove the excess fat, then toss into the lentils.

lentil, goat cheese & smoked meat salad
Prepare the basic recipe, adding 12 ounces chopped smoked ham and/or chicken to the lentils.

lentil & mozzarella salad
Prepare the basic recipe, replacing the goat cheese with a ball of mozzarella (buffalo mozzarella is best), ripped into pieces. For the dressing, replace the thyme with marjoram or basil.

lentil, goat cheese & antipasto salad
Prepare the basic recipe, replacing the onion, bell pepper, cucumber, and avocado with 1 (10-ounce) jar mixed antipasto salad, drained (or a combination of jarred grilled red peppers, mushrooms, and artichokes). For the dressing, simply stir in 1–2 tablespoons balsamic vinegar to taste — the vegetables will be well seasoned.

variations

mediterranean halloumi salad

see base recipe page 73

halloumi salad with lime & caper vinaigrette
Prepare the basic recipe, using a dressing made from the zest and juice of
1 lime, 2 tablespoons olive oil, 1 minced garlic clove, 1 tablespoon white wine
vinegar, 1 tablespoon capers, 1 teaspoon Dijon mustard, 1 tablespoon chopped
fresh cilantro, and salt and black pepper to taste.

halloumi salad with lentils
Prepare the basic recipe, replacing the garbanzo beans with 2 (15-ounce) cans
of lentils.

instant halloumi garbanzo salad
Prepare the basic recipe, omitting the cooked onion. Instead, finely slice a small
red onion and add to the garbanzo beans with the tomatoes. Make the
dressing by combining the olive oil, 2 tablespoons of white-wine vinegar only,
and the sugar, minced garlic, and chopped chile.

smoked paprika halloumi & garbanzo salad
Prepare the basic recipe for the salad. Combine 3 tablespoons flour and
1/2 teaspoon smoked paprika on a plate with a pinch of salt and black pepper.
Heat 2 tablespoons olive oil in a skillet. Dip the halloumi into the flour, shake
off the excess, and fry over medium heat, 2 minutes per side.

variations

german-style potato salad with sausage

see base recipe page 74

herbed creamy potato sausage salad
Prepare the basic recipe. For the dressing, combine 1/2 cup mayonnaise and
1/2 cup sour cream in a bowl, and stir in the mustard, salt, and pepper.

potato salad with sausage, eggs & dill pickles
Prepare the basic recipe, adding 1 or 2 chopped dill pickles and 1 tablespoon of
liquid from the pickle jar to the salad. Make 4 hard-boiled eggs. Cut into
quarters and serve on top of the salad. The sausage may be omitted for a
vegetarian potato salad.

potato salad with crab
Prepare the basic recipe, replacing the sausage with 1 (6-ounce) can of
crabmeat.

lemony-mustard potato sausage salad
Prepare the basic recipe. For the dressing, replace the wine vinegar with
3 tablespoons lemon juice and add the zest of 1 lemon.

german-style potato salad with sausage & sauerkraut
Prepare the basic recipe, adding 1 cup sauerkraut to the cooked potatoes and
sausage.

sandwiches

The most flexible meal, great for lunch away from home, a snack, or a quick supper. Sandwiches have so much creative potential — the following are just a few ideas to get your juices flowing.

hot beef sandwiches

see variations page 96

This is a hearty meal sandwich.

8 oz. beef round tip steak, about 1/4-in. thick
1 tbsp. olive oil
1 garlic clove, minced
1 1/2 tbsp. soy sauce
black pepper

1/2 medium red onion, sliced
2 oz. mushrooms, sliced
2 tbsp. red wine or water
1 tsp. Dijon mustard
4 Kaiser rolls or mini baguettes

Cut the steak in half, then into 1-inch strips, slicing across the grain. Heat the olive oil in a skillet, then add the beef and garlic and stir-fry until the meat is browned, about 2 minutes. Put in a dish with the soy sauce and black pepper, toss, and keep warm.

Using the same skillet, stir-fry the onion until soft, about 4 minutes, then add the mushrooms and cook until tender, about 3 minutes. Add the wine or water, mustard, and beef mixture. Bring to a boil, heat through, then divide the mixture among the rolls.

Serves 4

chicken lettuce wraps

see variations page 97

These are healthful and full of flavor. Allowing everyone to construct their own wrap makes this an easy meal option. Buying a package of stir-fry vegetables makes the shopping simple and cuts down on prep time. Cooking with jars or tubes of fresh ginger and garlic is a handy prep shortcut, too.

1 tbsp. sunflower or peanut oil
1 lb. ground chicken or turkey
1 tsp. minced garlic
1 tsp. minced fresh ginger
1 package stir-fry vegetable mix
6 tbsp. teriyaki sauce

2 tbsp. peanut butter
8–12 large iceberg lettuce leaves
2 green onions, thinly sliced
1/4 cup chopped fresh cilantro
hoisin sauce, for dipping

Heat the oil in a wok or large skillet and stir-fry the ground chicken or turkey, garlic, and ginger until the chicken is cooked through, about 5 minutes. Add the vegetable mix and stir-fry for about 3 minutes, or as directed on the package. Add the teriyaki sauce and peanut butter and cook for 2 minutes.

Transfer the stir-fry to a large platter and serve alongside the lettuce, green onions, and cilantro. Allow everyone to construct their own wrap. Serve hoisin sauce on the side for dipping.

Serves 4

roasted mushroom & goat cheese sandwiches

see variations page 98

Meaty mushrooms make a great base for a vegetarian sandwich that's equally good hot or cold.

1 lb. portobello mushrooms, cleaned and cut
    into 1/4-inch slices
1 tsp. dried thyme
2 tbsp. olive oil
4 Kaiser, ciabatta, or hamburger rolls, split

1 tbsp. lemon juice
2 oz. soft goat cheese, crumbled
salt and pepper
1/2 small red onion, finely sliced
2 cups mixed green leaves or arugula

Preheat oven to 375°F. Toss together the mushrooms, thyme, and oil. Put on a rimmed baking sheet and roast for 10 minutes, toss, then continue to roast until tender, 5 to 10 more minutes. A few minutes before the mushrooms are cooked, put the rolls on a separate baking sheet and heat in the oven, cut side up. Sprinkle the mushrooms with lemon juice, then put the crumbled goat cheese on top and allow to melt.

Transfer the mushrooms onto the warm rolls, season generously with salt and pepper, and top with the red onion and mixed greens or arugula.

Serves 4

tortilla chicken pizzas

see variations page 99

Mealtimes couldn't be easier or quicker. Play around with the toppings to suit your family's whims.

1 tsp. olive oil
4 flour tortillas
1 cup shredded cooked chicken
2 tbsp. BBQ sauce
1 large tomato, sliced

1 small red onion, finely sliced
8 black olives
salt and black pepper
1 (4-oz.) ball mozzarella, torn
2 tbsp. Parmesan cheese, to serve

Preheat oven to 400°F. Heat the olive oil in a skillet and cook the tortillas for a few minutes until firm. Do not overcook.

Place the tortillas on a baking sheet. Mix together the chicken and BBQ sauce; divide among the tortillas. Distribute the other ingredients over the top. Bake for 5–10 minutes, or until the cheese is melted, taking care not to over-brown the outside of the tortillas. Sprinkle the cooked pizza with Parmesan cheese.

Serves 4

grilled caprese sandwiches

see variations page 100

This sandwich is inspired by insalata Caprese, the colorful Italian salad consisting of mozzarella, ripe tomatoes, and fresh basil.

1 tbsp. butter
4 thick slices of bread
1 (4-oz.) ball mozzarella, sliced
1 large tomato, sliced
whole basil leaves

1/2 avocado, sliced
1 tsp. lemon juice
salt and black pepper
balsamic vinegar

Butter the bread. Put the mozzarella slices on the unbuttered side of two slices of bread. Top with tomato slices and whole basil leaves. Toss the avocado with the lemon juice to prevent discoloration and put on top of the tomato. Season with salt and pepper and drizzle with a little balsamic vinegar. Put the other slices of bread on top, buttered side up.

Fry in a hot skillet, pressing down with a spatula until golden brown on both sides. The cheese should be melting. Alternatively, cook in a sandwich toaster. Cut each sandwich in half and eat at once.

Serves 2

sunshine pita pockets

see variations page 101

These sandwiches are great for Sunday brunch and bring a ray of sunshine to even the dullest day.

1 tbsp. butter
2 eggs, lightly beaten
salt and black pepper
4 pita breads

3 oz. cream cheese
1 large tomato, thinly sliced
2 green onions, sliced
2 oz. alfalfa sprouts

Melt the butter in a skillet. Season the beaten egg with salt and pepper, then add to the pan and cook over medium heat until the egg has set; remove from the heat.

Meanwhile, cut the pita breads in half width-wise and gently open them up. Spread with cream cheese and top with tomato slices and green onions. Slice the egg into strips and put into the pockets. Stuff with the alfalfa sprouts.

Serves 4

pimento cheese sandwiches

see variations page 102

A classic, southern comfort food. The mixture keeps in the refrigerator for several days, so make a large batch if you have friends coming; that way, you've got an instant sandwich filler or cracker topping on hand when hunger strikes.

4 oz. jarred pimentos, drained
8 oz. sharp cheddar cheese, shredded
2 tbsp. mayonnaise
2 tbsp. Greek yogurt
1/2 tsp. red pepper flakes
1/2 tsp. Worcestershire sauce

1 tbsp. prepared horseradish, optional
pinch cayenne
1 tsp. lemon juice
salt and pepper
8 slices artisan white bread

Dry the pimentos with paper towels, then finely chop. Put in a medium bowl with the next nine ingredients, adjusting the seasoning and spices to taste.

Make the sandwiches with the sliced bread, spreading the pimento cheese generously.

Serves 4

trout & beet sandwiches

see variations page 103

These delicate sandwiches are perfect for a light meal or a picnic. If you don't have trout, the sandwiches are just as delicious with smoked salmon.

4 oz. cream cheese
2 tbsp. sour cream
1 tsp. prepared horseradish
6 medium beets, cut into matchsticks

8–12 slices whole wheat bread, crusts removed
2 tbsp. butter
4 oz. boneless, skinned smoked trout
2 tbsp. chopped fresh dill or chives

In a bowl, combine the cream cheese, sour cream, horseradish, and beets. Lay half the bread slices down on a board, butter them, then divide the trout among them. Top with the beet mixture and dill or chives, and cover with the remaining bread. Cut into triangles to serve.

Serves 4

variations

hot beef sandwiches

see base recipe page 85

hot beef gyros
Prepare the basic recipe, omitting mushrooms, red wine, mustard, and rolls.
Prepare a tzatziki using 1 cup Greek yogurt, 1/4 cup diced cucumber,
1 tablespoon chopped fresh dill, and salt and pepper to taste. Stuff hot beef
and tzatziki into pita bread.

beef & blue sandwiches
Prepare the basic recipe, omitting mushrooms, red wine, and mustard. In a
small bowl, crumble 2 ounces Stilton or Roquefort cheese and mix with
1/2 cup sour cream and 2 tablespoons mayonnaise. Spread over the base of
the rolls before adding the beef. Add slices of tomato, if desired.

beef & pepperdew sandwiches
Prepare the beef and blue sandwiches as directed above, adding 2 or 3 sliced
pepperdew peppers to each sandwich.

wasabi beef sandwiches
Prepare the basic recipe, omitting mushrooms, red wine, and Dijon mustard.
Add 2 tablespoons grainy mustard, 2 teaspoons honey, and 1/2–1 teaspoon
wasabi paste to the cooked beef and onions.

chicken lettuce wraps

see base recipe page 86

pork lettuce wraps
Prepare the basic recipe, replacing the chicken with 1 pound ground pork. Drain off any excess fat before adding vegetables.

asian raw vegetable wraps
Prepare the basic recipe, using only 2 tablespoons teriyaki sauce. Serve with a selection of raw vegetables (shredded carrot, sliced mushrooms, sliced red bell pepper, mung bean sprouts, shredded Chinese cabbage, bean sprouts, baby corn).

shrimp asian wraps
Prepare the basic recipe, replacing the chicken with 1 pound small shelled and deveined shrimp.

asian tortilla wraps
Prepare the basic recipe. Put a lettuce leaf on top of each of 4 tortillas. Top with the stir-fry mix and top with another lettuce leaf. Roll up the tortillas tightly and cut each in half diagonally to serve.

roasted mushroom & goat cheese sandwiches

see base recipe page 87

mushroom melts
Prepare the basic recipe, omitting the goat cheese. Do not slice the mushroom, but toss in oil, sprinkle with thyme, then put a slice of mozzarella or Monterey Jack cheese in the mushroom cavity.

mushroom & blue cheese sandwiches
Prepare the basic recipe, replacing the goat cheese with crumbled blue cheese such as Roquefort or the milder dolcelatte.

mushroom & avocado sandwiches
Prepare the basic recipe, but toss 1 sliced avocado in the lemon juice and place on top of the cheese in the sandwiches.

balsamic mushroom & apple sandwiches
Prepare the basic recipe, replacing the lemon juice with balsamic vinegar. Complete the sandwiches using a slice of cheddar or Monterey Jack cheese in place of goat cheese and topping each with two slices of apple (dipped in lemon juice to prevent discoloration, if not serving immediately).

tortilla chicken pizzas

see base recipe page 88

tortilla egg pizzas
Prepare the basic recipe, omitting the chicken. Spread 1 teaspoon pesto onto
each tortilla, and top with the remaining ingredients. Break an egg into the
center of each pizza and bake in the oven until the egg is cooked as desired.

spinach tortilla pizzas
Prepare the basic recipe, omitting the chicken. Spread each tortilla with
1 teaspoon pesto and top with the remaining ingredients and 1 (10-ounce)
package frozen spinach, thawed and squeezed dry.

spicy tortilla pizza mexicali
Prepare the basic recipe, replacing the BBQ sauce with 1 teaspoon dry taco
seasoning mix. Top with the remaining ingredients as well as 1/4 cup each of
canned corn and black beans and a sliced jalapeño. Garnish with chopped
cilantro and dollops of sour cream.

flatbread pizzas
Prepare the basic recipe or any of the variations above, replacing the tortillas
with a Middle Eastern flatbread.

variations

grilled caprese sandwiches

see base recipe page 91

grilled camembert & grape jelly sandwiches
Prepare the basic recipe, omitting the tomato, basil, and avocado, and
replacing the mozzarella with Camembert cheese. Put 1 tablespoon grape
jelly or cranberry sauce on top of the cheese.

grilled italian cheese & ham sandwiches
Prepare the basic recipe, omitting the avocado and basil. Use either
mozzarella or taleggio cheese. Put 1 slice Italian-style ham on top of the
cheese, then top with tomato.

grilled cheddar & chutney sandwiches
Prepare the basic recipe, omitting the avocado and basil, and replacing the
mozzarella with cheddar cheese. Put 1 tablespoon apple chutney on top of
the cheese. The tomato is optional.

egg-dipped swiss sandwiches
Prepare the basic recipe, but do not butter the outside of the bread. Omit
the avocado and basil, and replace the mozzarella with Swiss cheese. In a
wide bowl, lightly beat 1 egg with 1 tablespoon milk. Dip the sandwiches in
the egg, covering well. Pan-fry the sandwiches as directed.

variations

sunshine pita pockets

see base recipe page 92

italian sunshine sandwiches
Prepare the basic recipe, replacing cream cheese and alfafa with ricotta cheese and arugula.

goat cheese sunshine sandwiches
Prepare the basic recipe, replacing cream cheese with soft goat cheese.

grilled pepper & jalapeño sunshine sandwiches
Prepare the basic recipe, replacing tomato with 2 charbroiled peppers and adding a seeded thinly sliced jalapeño chile.

breakfast sunshine sandwiches
Prepare the basic recipe, but before cooking the egg, pan-fry 4 strips of bacon. Omit butter and salt, and fry the egg in the bacon fat before continuing as directed. Crumble the fried bacon and stuff into the pita with the egg.

variations

pimento cheese sandwiches

see base recipe page 94

pimento cheeseburgers
Prepare the basic recipe, omitting the bread. Season 4 hamburger patties with salt and pepper. Broil burgers under a pre-heated broiler, turning once, until cooked as desired. Spread 2 tablespoons pimento cheese over each burger; return to the heat and let melt. Serve burgers on buns with lettuce and tomato.

pimento cheese & turkey sandwiches
Prepare the basic recipe, adding slices of turkey to the sandwiches.

hot pimento cheese appetizer dip
Prepare the basic recipe, omitting the bread. Place the bowl of pimento cheese in the microwave and cook for 30 seconds at a time, until just melted. Serve as an appetizer with celery, carrot, and cucumber sticks, along with slices of bell pepper and crackers or bread sticks.

pimento-cheese potato skins
Prepare the basic recipe, omitting the bread. Remove the flesh from 8 baked potatoes, leaving 1/4-inch layer. Brush all over with olive oil. Bake in a 400°F oven for 7 minutes, flip, then bake for 5 minutes. Fill with pimento cheese and cook for 5 minutes. Serve with bacon bits, sour cream, and chives.

variations

trout & beet sandwiches

see base recipe page 95

smoked trout, horseradish & cucumber on rye
Prepare the basic recipe, omitting beet and replacing whole-wheat
bread with rye. Top the cream cheese mixture with thin slices of peeled
cucumber.

smoked salmon & watercress sandwiches
Prepare the basic recipe, using smoked salmon and omitting beet and
horseradish. Add 1/4 cup chopped watercress to the cream cheese mixture with
1 teaspoon lemon juice. Top with watercress leaves.

danish-style smoked trout open-face sandwiches
Prepare the basic recipe, omitting butter and replacing whole-wheat bread
with pumpernickel or multi-seeded bread. Spread the bread with beet mixture,
and top with trout and a little fresh dill or chives.

smoked trout and egg sandwiches
Prepare the basic recipe, replacing beet and horseradish in cream cheese
mixture with 1 small shredded carrot; 2 tablespoons each of fine chopped
celery, green onions, and capers; 1/2 teaspoon lemon zest; and 1 teaspoon
lemon juice. Spread on the bread and top with the trout, slices of egg from
2 hard-boiled eggs, and dill or chives. Cover with second slice of bread.

poultry

Poultry is the quick cook's best friend — and chicken and turkey are healthy choices. Sliced boneless chicken, turkey, or duck can be cooked in just a few minutes, and even a chicken leg can be grilled in about 20 minutes.

grilled chicken with lemon & thyme

see variations page 120

Grilled chicken makes a perfect supper and is loved by almost everyone. The directions here work for an outside grill as well as a broiler; either way, with a bit of basting with an aromatic oil or butter, it'll be delicious. This dish can be prepared partly in advance; the chicken and marinade can be kept in a resealable plastic bag in the refrigerator for up to 24 hours.

for the marinade
3 tbsp. olive oil
1 1/2 tbsp. lemon juice
zest from 1/2 lemon
1 garlic clove, minced, or 1 tsp. garlic powder

1 tbsp. chopped fresh thyme or 1 tsp.
    dried thyme
salt and black pepper

4 chicken breasts, skin on

In a large bowl, combine the olive oil, lemon juice and zest, garlic, thyme, and salt and pepper to taste. Add the chicken and turn to coat.

Cook the chicken on the grill or a under the broiler about 4 inches away from the heat. Cook for about 12–15 minutes, turning halfway through cooking time and basting frequently with the remaining oil mixture. When the chicken is cooked, it will feel firm and springy to the touch and the juices will run clear.

Serves 4

chicken chow mein

see variations page 121

This is such an easy dish to cook in a hurry. Use a dark soy sauce for a rich flavor or light soy sauce for a brighter taste. If desired, you can use other vegetables such as snow peas, bamboo shoots, zucchini, or thin green beans and thinly sliced carrots blanched for 1 minute before stir-frying.

10 oz. medium egg noodles
sesame seed oil
1 lb. skinless chicken meat, cut into strips
2 tbsp. cornstarch
1/3 cup soy sauce
2 tsp. Chinese five-spice powder
2 tsp. chili sauce

2–4 tbsp. sunflower oil
1 red bell pepper, finely sliced
1 green bell pepper, finely sliced
4 oz. white cabbage, shredded
8 oz. bean sprouts
4 green onions, sliced on the diagonal
freshly ground black pepper

Cook the noodles in a saucepan of boiling water for 2–3 minutes until just cooked through, or follow the package directions, if different. Drain, then toss with a little sesame oil to keep the noodles from sticking. Keep warm.

Meanwhile, put the chicken in a bowl and coat in the cornstarch. Stir in 2 tablespoons soy sauce, five-spice powder, and chili sauce.

Heat the oil in a wok or very large skillet until very hot, then add the chicken and stir-fry for 3–5 minutes until the chicken is golden brown and cooked through. Transfer to a plate and keep warm. Maintaining the heat in the wok, add the peppers and stir-fry for 1 minute, then add the cabbage and stir-fry for 1 minute. Add the bean sprouts and green onions, and stir-

fry for 1 additional minute. Return the chicken to the wok along with the noodles. Add a generous grinding of black pepper, a dash of sesame oil, and sufficient soy sauce to coat the vegetables and noodles. Serve immediately.

Serves 4

chicken with tangerine & chipotle sauce

see variations page 122

This is one of those dishes that tastes incredibly sophisticated, but has minimal ingredients — it couldn't be simpler. Serve with a side of plain rice and some black beans. It is a great recipe to make when there are some past-their-best tangerines in the fruit bowl.

1 tbsp. sunflower oil
4 skinless boneless chicken breasts
1 1/4 cup tangerine juice (from 5–6 tangerines)
2–3 canned chipotle chiles

2–3 tbsp. adobo sauce
pinch of salt
fresh cilantro, to garnish

Preheat a heavy skillet, just big enough to hold the chicken pieces, over medium heat for 2 minutes. Add the oil, then the chicken; cook on each side for 1 minute to seal. Add the tangerine juice, chipotles, adobo sauce, and salt. Simmer over medium heat for 8–12 minutes, depending on the thickness of the meat. Turn the chicken halfway through cooking time and add a little more juice if the sauce starts to dry out. Check that the chicken is cooked through by making a small insertion with a sharp knife and ensuring that the flesh is completely white. Serve drizzled with sauce and garnished with cilantro.

Serves 4

chicken–corn burgers with cumin & ginger

see variations page 123

The corn and spices give a novel twist to the chicken burger. Serve on a bun with lettuce and cucumber, and a tomato or Thai chili sauce. The burgers can be cooked from frozen, so double up the recipe and keep some as a standby.

1 lb. ground chicken
1 cup breadcrumbs made from stale bread
1 egg
1 cup canned corn
1 tbsp. soy sauce
2 green onions, finely chopped

2 tsp. ground cumin
1 tsp. fresh ginger, finely chopped
1 garlic clove, minced
pinch chili powder
1 tbsp. oil

In a large bowl, combine all the ingredients except the oil; this is easiest done with your hands. Shape the mixture into 4 large or 6 medium patties.

Heat the oil in a heavy skillet, then pan-fry over medium heat for 10–12 minutes, turning once, until cooked through. Alternatively, these burgers may be cooked on the grill.

Serves 4–6

chicken in mustard cream sauce

see variations page 124

This will soon become the quick dish that you serve to impress. Poaching the chicken in vermouth makes it moist, rich, and slightly scented; you could substitute a good-flavored white wine such as chardonnay, and the resulting dish will still be delicious. All you need are some new potatoes and a steamed green vegetable, such as broccoli or spinach, on the side.

4 skinless boneless chicken breasts
about 1 cup dry vermouth
1/4 cup heavy cream

2 tbsp. grainy mustard
salt and pepper

Put the chicken breasts in a saucepan that is just big enough to hold them in one layer. Pour the vermouth over them, making sure that the chicken is covered; you may need a little more if the pan is large. Bring to a boil to over medium heat, skimming off any residue that might rise to the surface. Reduce the heat; cover and simmer for 15 minutes, or until the chicken is cooked through. Remove the chicken and keep warm.

Increase the heat and boil the vermouth for a few minutes until there is about 1/2 cup remaining and it has become syrupy. Add the cream, mustard, and salt and pepper to taste. Pour over the chicken and serve.

Serves 4

chicken puttanesca with couscous

see variations page 125

This Italian classic with its bright flavors is a great quick and healthy supper dish that the whole family is sure to love. Don't be put off by a longer-than-usual ingredients list — you simply toss it all in! Here it is paired with a simple orange-scented couscous, but it is equally good with pasta or pan-fried, ready-to-cook polenta slices.

for the puttanesca sauce
1 tbsp. olive oil
4 skinless boneless chicken breasts
salt and black pepper
1 1/4 cups chicken broth
1 (15-oz.) can chopped tomatoes
2 cups (10 oz.) frozen pearl onions
2 carrots, chopped
1 cup frozen peas
16 black olives, pitted

1 tbsp. capers
1/2 tsp. garlic powder
1 tbsp. fresh oregano, chopped
1/4 cup basil leaves, chopped

for the couscous
1 cup couscous
1 1/4 cups water
zest of 1/2 orange
1 tbsp. orange juice

Heat the oil in a large skillet. Season the chicken with salt and pepper to taste, then place in skillet and cook over medium-high heat for 1 minute on each side to seal and brown. Add the remaining ingredients for the sauce except the basil. Bring to a boil, then reduce the heat to a simmer. Cook, stirring occasionally, for 10–12 minutes or until the chicken is cooked through.

Meanwhile, bring 1 1/4 cups water to a boil in a small saucepan. Pour in the couscous, stir with a fork, cover, and set aside for 5 minutes. Fluff with a fork and stir in the orange zest and juice.

Add the basil to the sauce and adjust the seasoning to taste. Serve over the couscous.

Serves 4

stir-fry turkey with peppers

see variations page 126

The quick stir-frying of the peppers ensures that much of their vitamin C survives the cooking process. If you plan to cook this for supper, you may wish to marinate the turkey in the soy and Worcestershire sauces in the morning, and leave covered in the refrigerator. Serve over plain rice.

1 lb. turkey meat, sliced
3 tbsp. soy sauce
3 tbsp. Worcestershire sauce
3 tbsp. oil

1 medium green bell pepper, deseeded and sliced
1 medium red bell pepper, deseeded and sliced
4 oz. cremini mushrooms, sliced

Put the turkey meat in a bowl with the soy and Worcestershire sauces and stir to mix. Set aside for 10 minutes. Drain off the liquid and reserve.

Heat the oil in a wok or large skillet and add the turkey. Stir-fry over medium heat for about 5 minutes, until cooked through. Remove and keep warm.

Stir-fry the green and red pepper slices in the same pan for 2 minutes, then add the mushrooms and cook until the mushrooms are almost tender. Return the turkey to the pan with the reserved marinade and cook for 1–2 minutes to heat through.

Serves 4

thai green chicken curry

see variations page 127

This fragrant and creamy Thai-style curry is stunning served with sticky jasmine rice.
When cooked, mold the rice into a pasta bowl using a 1/2 measuring cup as a scoop, and
serve surrounded by the curry.

4 oz. green beans
1 tbsp. sunflower oil
4 oz. snow peas
1 red bell pepper, deseeded and sliced
1 garlic clove, minced
4 skinless boneless chicken breasts or thighs,
    sliced into bite-size pieces

1–1 1/2 tbsp. Thai green curry paste
1 (14-oz.) can coconut milk
2 tsp. fish sauce
1 tsp. sugar
3 wide strips of lime zest
1/4 cup Thai basil leaves, torn

In a small saucepan, blanch the green beans for 2 minutes. In a wok or large skillet, heat the
sunflower oil and stir-fry the snow peas for 1 minute. Add the drained green beans and stir-
fry for 1 minute. Add the bell pepper and stir-fry for 2 minutes. Remove the vegetables and
keep warm.

Add the chicken to the same skillet and stir-fry until it has turned white all over. Add the
garlic to the pan and stir-fry for 30 seconds, then add the curry paste to taste and cook for
1 minute. Pour in the coconut milk, fish sauce, sugar, and lime zest, and bring almost to a
boil, then simmer for 5 minutes or until the chicken is cooked through. Return the
vegetables to the pan and warm through. Remove the lime zest, stir in the basil, and
serve immediately.

Serves 4

chicken with creamy red pesto sauce

see variations page 128

What a delicious chicken dish — and so simple! If making for company, you could prepare to the point where the chicken is cooked in the sauce and set aside. Reheat while cooking pasta, rice, or polenta, then add the sour cream and finish. Fusilli pasta is used in the recipe below.

1 tbsp. olive oil
1 small red onion, thinly sliced
3 chicken breasts, diced
1/3 cup jarred sundried tomato pesto
1/2 cup chicken broth or white wine

4 oz. mushrooms, sliced
12 oz. dried fusilli
1/2 cup sour cream or crème fraîche
salt and black pepper
Parmesan cheese, to serve

Heat the oil in a skillet over medium heat. Add the red onion and cook for 5 minutes, until softened. Add the diced chicken and cook for 2 minutes, until evenly white. Add the pesto and broth or wine; bring to a boil. Add the mushrooms, cover, then simmer for 15 minutes, or until the chicken is cooked through. Increase the heat and reduce the liquid by one-third. Stir in the sour cream or crème fraîche and heat through without boiling, then add salt and pepper to taste. Serve over pasta, rice, or polenta, sprinkled with the Parmesan cheese.

Serves 4

herbed cheese–stuffed chicken breasts

see variations page 129

The cream cheese flavors and moistens the chicken breasts as they cook, making this dish worthy of the finest company. The chicken breasts can be stuffed in advance, so this dish is great for a large party. Just serve with potatoes and steamed green beans or a green salad.

4 chicken breasts, skin on
4 oz. cream cheese with herbs and garlic
8 slices prosciutto or other air-dried ham

small bunch vine-ripened cherry tomatoes
2 tbsp. water
juice of 1/2 lemon

Preheat the oven to 400°F. Put the chicken breasts on a board; gently loosen and lift the skin without detaching it. Put a spoonful of the cream cheese under the skin of each breast. Wrap a slice of prosciutto tightly around each to keep the filling enclosed.

Transfer to a roasting pan, add the tomatoes still on the stem, then cook in the oven for about 20 minutes, until cooked through. Remove the chicken and tomatoes to the serving dish and keep warm. Add the water and lemon juice to the roasting pan and stir over the heat to deglaze, scraping off any crispy bits. Spoon the juices over the chicken.

Serves 4

grilled chicken with lemon & thyme

see base recipe page 105

cajun spiced grilled chicken
Prepare the basic recipe, replacing the lemon juice, zest, and thyme with
1 tablespoon paprika, 1 teaspoon cayenne pepper, and 2 tablespoons fresh
oregano (or 2 teaspoons dried).

honey-mustard chicken
Prepare the basic recipe, replacing the lemon juice, zest, and thyme with
3 tablespoons each of honey, sunflower oil, and grainy mustard, and
1 tablespoon balsamic vinegar.

teriyaki chicken
Prepare the basic recipe, replacing the lemon juice, zest, and thyme with
1 cup teriyaki sauce, 2 tablespoons lemon juice, 1 minced garlic clove,
2 teaspoons sesame oil, and a few drops of Tabasco.

harissa grilled chicken
Prepare the basic recipe, replacing the lemon juice, zest, and thyme with
4 tablespoons harissa paste and 1 tablespoon each of cumin seeds (which
have been dry-toasted for 1 minute), lemon juice, and olive oil.

variations

chicken chow mein

see base recipe page 106

pork chow mein
Prepare the basic recipe, replacing the chicken with 1 pound boneless pork loin or ground pork. Drain off all but 1 tablespoon of fat before cooking the vegetables.

tofu chow mein
Prepare the basic recipe, replacing the chicken with 1 pound extra-firm tofu, which has been pressed, drained, and cut into 1/2-inch pieces. Smoked tofu can also be used in this recipe.

gluten-free chow mein
Prepare the basic recipe, using gluten-free rice noodle sticks, gluten-free rice, or quinoa-based linguine or spaghetti. Cook according to package directions.

stir-fry chicken & vegetables
Prepare the basic recipe, omitting the noodles. Serve the chicken and vegetables on a bed of plain fried rice or egg fried rice.

chicken with tangerine & chipotle sauce

see base recipe page 109

seared tuna with tangerine & chipotle sauce

Prepare the basic recipe using 4 tuna steaks in place of the chicken. Rub the olive oil and a little salt directly into the steaks. Cook on each side for 1–2 minutes depending on the thickness of the steak; seared tuna is best medium rare. Add the remaining ingredients to the skillet and cook for 2–3 minutes until the liquid is reduced by a third. Serve the sauce over the tuna.

duck with tangerine & chipotle sauce

Prepare the basic recipe, replacing the chicken with 4 small boneless duck breasts, skin on. Lightly score the duck breasts and season with salt. Cook on the first side until the skin is really crisp, 8–10 minutes, depending on thickness of the breast; drain off excess fat. Add the remaining ingredients and cook the second side for 5–10 minutes until the duck is almost cooked through; duck is best very slightly undercooked in the center.

chicken in orange & sweet chili sauce

Prepare the basic recipe, omitting the chipotle in adobo sauce and replacing the tangerine juice with orange juice. With the orange juice add 1/2 cup chili sauce, 1 tablespoon each of brown sugar and soy sauce, and 1 teaspoon each of Dijon mustard and garlic powder.

chicken–corn burgers with cumin & ginger

see base recipe page 110

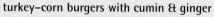

turkey–corn burgers with cumin & ginger
Prepare the basic recipe, replacing the chicken with ground turkey.

chicken–corn burgers with tomato & basil
Prepare the basic recipe, replacing the cumin, ginger, and chili with
1 tablespoon tomato paste and 2 tablespoons fresh chopped basil.

chicken & feta burgers
Prepare the basic recipe, omitting corn and ginger, and using only 1/2 teaspoon
cumin. Add 6 ounces crumbled feta cheese and 1/2 teaspoon dried oregano.

jalapeño–lime chicken & corn burgers
Prepare the basic recipe, replacing the cumin, ginger, and chile with grated lime
zest and 2 tablespoons lime juice, 1 finely chopped deseeded jalapeño chile,
2 tablespoons fresh chopped cilantro, and a pinch of sugar.

variations

chicken in mustard cream sauce

see base recipe page 111

low-fat, lactose-free chicken in mustard cream sauce
Prepare the basic recipe, replacing the heavy cream with nondairy,
soy-based cream.

chicken in tarragon sauce
Prepare the basic recipe, replacing the mustard with 2 tablespoons fresh
chopped tarragon.

chicken in garlic cream sauce
Prepare the basic recipe, adding 2–3 minced garlic cloves to the poaching
chicken and omitting the grainy mustard. However, you can combine the
two and make a garlicky mustard cream sauce.

tilapia in vermouth with creamy mustard sauce
Prepare the basic recipe, replacing the chicken with tilapia fillets. Poach
for 5 minutes until the fish is opaque and beginning to flake. Proceed as
directed or follow the tarragon sauce option above.

variations

chicken puttanesca with couscous

see base recipe page 112

pork chop puttanesca with couscous
Prepare the basic recipe, replacing the chicken with pork chops. The cooking
time may need to be increased by a few minutes, depending on the thickness
of the meat.

vegetarian puttanesca with couscous
Prepare the basic recipe, omitting the chicken and olive oil. Cook the sauce in a
saucepan, adding 1 (15-ounce) can garbanzo beans with the canned tomatoes,
for 10 minutes, or until the vegetables are tender.

leftover turkey puttanesca with couscous
Prepare the basic recipe, replacing the chicken with 1 pound chopped cooked
turkey meat (or other leftover cooked meat). There is no need to precook meat
in oil; simply add to the remaining ingredients and cook as directed.

swordfish puttanesca with couscous
Prepare the basic recipe, replacing the chicken with swordfish steaks. The
swordfish will be cooked in 5–8 minutes, depending on the thickness of the
steaks; do not overcook or they will become dry.

variations

stir-fry turkey with peppers

see base recipe page 114

stir-fry shrimp with peppers
Prepare the basic recipe, omitting the marinating process and replacing the turkey with 1 pound large peeled and deveined raw shrimp. Stir-fry for 5–7 minutes until cooked through, then proceed as directed.

stir-fry beef with peppers
Prepare the basic recipe, replacing the turkey with 1 pound lean beef steak, cut into thin strips across the grain. Stir-fry for 2 minutes or more to taste, then remove from the pan and proceed as directed.

stir-fry turkey with peppers & chard
Prepare the basic recipe, omitting the green bell pepper and mushrooms. Remove the stalks from 1 pound Swiss chard, roughly chop them, then stir-fry for 2 minutes with the red bell pepper. Add the shredded chard leaves and stir-fry for 1–2 minutes, until wilted and just tender. Proceed as directed.

stir-fry spicy chicken with peppers
Prepare the basic recipe, replacing the turkey with 1 pound sliced chicken meat and adding 1/2–1 teaspoon of hot sauce to the marinade.

variations

thai green chicken curry

see base recipe page 115

thai red chicken curry
Prepare the basic recipe, replacing the green Thai curry paste with red Thai curry paste. The former is based on green chiles, cilantro, galangal, and lemongrass; the latter has more red chile, garlic, and ginger.

thai vegetable & bean curry
Prepare the basic recipe, omitting the chicken. Add the garlic and green curry paste to the skillet, cook for 1 minute, then add 2 cups frozen edamame (soy beans) with the coconut milk.

thai vegetable & crispy tofu curry
Prepare the basic recipe, omitting the chicken. Take 1 pound pressed and drained extra-firm tofu and cut into bite-size pieces, and toss in 3 tablespoons of flour seasoned with salt, pepper, and garlic powder. In a separate skillet, heat 2 tablespoons sunflower oil and cook the tofu, turning from time to time until crisp. Toss into the finished curry and serve at once to retain crispiness.

thai pork curry
Prepare the basic recipe, replacing the chicken with 1 pound pork fillet, thinly sliced.

chicken with creamy red pesto sauce

see base recipe page 116

chicken with pesto & tomatoes

Prepare the basic recipe, omitting the mushrooms and replacing the sundried tomato pesto with 3 tablespoons green pesto. Add 8 ounces halved grape tomatoes to the cooked chicken and cook for a few minutes to soften before adding the sour cream.

chicken with creamy pesto–chili sauce

Prepare the basic recipe, adding 1 red chile, deseeded and thinly sliced, to the onion once it has cooked for 3 minutes. Continue to cook for 2 minutes. Proceed as directed.

creamy arugula pesto shrimp

Prepare the basic recipe, replacing the chicken and sundried tomato pesto with 1 pound large raw shrimp, peeled and deveined, and arugula pesto. Do not pre-fry the shrimp; simply add to the sauce and simmer for 10 minutes until cooked. Proceed as directed. Serve over linguine.

chicken with creamy red-pesto walnut sauce

Prepare the basic recipe, omitting the mushrooms. Dry-toast 1 cup walnut pieces in a skillet over medium heat for 3–5 minutes until just beginning to brown. Add to the chicken with the sour cream.

herbed cheese–stuffed chicken breasts

see base recipe page 119

italian stuffed chicken breasts
Prepare the basic recipe, carefully sliding 2 thin slices mozzarella, 2 whole basil leaves, and 1 quartered grape tomato under the skin of the chicken.

blue cheese & spinach–stuffed chicken breasts
Prepare the basic recipe, using 2 ounces plain cream cheese mixed with 2 ounces crumbled blue cheese. Squeeze liquid from 3 ounces thawed frozen spinach, and mix with the cheese. Use to stuff the chicken breasts.

herbed cheese–stuffed chicken breasts with roasted pepper sauce
Prepare the basic recipe, omitting the tomatoes and lemon juice. To make the sauce, combine in the pan 1 (10-ounce) jar of roasted red peppers, drained, with 1 cup canned tomatoes, 2 tablespoons red wine, and 1/2 crumbled vegetable bouillon cube. Bring to a boil and simmer 15 minutes. Remove from heat and purée with a stick blender or in the food processor. Serve hot with the chicken.

sausage-stuffed chicken breasts
Prepare the basic recipe, omitting the herbed cream cheese. Squeeze the sausage meat from the casings of 2 herbed sausages. Use to stuff the chicken breasts.

meat

Meat need not take ages to cook, but to do it

quickly and successfully it has to be a prime cut.

The following recipes are all quick and magnificently

easy to prepare.

medallions of pork with lemon & parsley

see variations page 144

Pork medallions will cook through in the time taken to brown them on the outside, so it's worth the extra time spent banging them with a rolling pin or mallet — or even the back of a skillet. Serve with simple mashed potatoes and steamed green beans.

1 pork tenderloin (about 1 lb.)
3 tbsp. olive oil
salt and black pepper
1/2 cup dry white wine

juice of 1 large lemon
2 tbsp. chopped fresh parsley
1 lemon, quartered

Cut the tenderloin into 1/4-inch slices. Put between 2 sheets of waxed paper and pound to make them about half their original width; you need to do this in batches, reusing the paper.

Heat the olive oil in a large skillet and, working in batches, add the slices in a single layer. Season with a little salt and pepper to taste, and cook until browned on both sides. Remove to a warm plate and keep warm. Repeat until all the pork is cooked.

Add the wine and deglaze by scraping any pork pieces from the base of the skillet; allow to bubble until there is just a little wine left. Add the lemon juice and parsley, return the meat to the pan and stir, working quickly to coat all of the meat in the lemon juice. Serve immediately with extra lemon wedges.

Serves 4

steak with horseradish butter

see variations page 145

Beef and horseradish are a classic combination; both work well with beets, so serve with a beet salad or a potato salad (see page 74). The flavored butter can be made in advance and kept in the refrigerator, or can be made in bulk and kept in the freezer until needed.

for the horseradish butter
4 oz. butter, softened
2 tbsp. prepared horseradish sauce
1/2 tbsp. Dijon mustard
1 tbsp. fresh chopped parsley

for the steaks
4 6-8 oz. rump or rib-eye steaks,
   1- to 1 1/4-in. thick
1–2 tbsp. olive oil
black pepper

Preheat a broiler, grill, or griddle to high.

For the horseradish butter, mash together the butter, horseradish, mustard, and parsley. Alternately, prepare in a food processor. Put on a piece of plastic wrap and shape into a roll. Put in the freezer to quickly chill (or put in the refrigerator if not using immediately). Note: If using sweet butter, add a pinch or two of sea salt to taste.

Brush each steak lightly with olive oil and grind a little black pepper on top. Cook for 3 minutes each side for medium rare, or more or less to each person's preference. Let rest for 3 minutes before serving. Top with the horseradish butter.

Serves 4

gingered beef & broccoli stir-fry

see variations page 146

Chinese-style cooking is terrific when time is short. For best results, slice the flank steak in half along the grain, then into thin strips across the grain. Freezing the steak for 15 minutes also makes it easier to cut. Serve with plain or egg fried rice, or egg noodles.

1 lb. lean flank steak, finely sliced
1 tsp. Chinese five-spice powder
1 tbsp. cornstarch
12 oz. broccoli, cut into florets and halved
1/4 cup light soy sauce
1 tsp. honey or corn syrup

1 tbsp. rice wine vinegar or red wine vinegar
3 tbsp. oil, preferably peanut
1 garlic clove, minced
1-inch piece fresh ginger, finely sliced
3 green onions, sliced on the diagonal
black pepper

Pat the beef dry with a paper towel, then sprinkle with five-spice powder and cornstarch, and toss lightly. Blanch the broccoli in boiling water for 1 minute, then remove from the water and set aside, reserving the water. In a small bowl, mix the soy sauce, honey, rice wine vinegar or red wine vinegar, and 3 tablespoons reserved water.

Heat the oil in a wok or large sauté pan over high heat until nearly smoking. Working in batches, sauté the beef till just browned, about 1 minute. Transfer to a bowl and keep warm.

Put the garlic into the wok and stir-fry for 30–45 seconds. Add the ginger and cook for 30–45 seconds. Add the broccoli and stir-fry for 2–3 minutes, until the broccoli is tender-crisp. Return the beef to the wok, add green onions and the soy sauce mixture, then cook for 2 minutes, adding a little more reserved water, if necessary, if the sauce becomes too thick.
Serves 4

instant frank & beans pot

see variations page 147

Sometimes a pantry meal is a godsend. Simply serve in a bowl with bread or crackers.

1 (15 oz.) can navy beans
1 (15 oz.) can kidney beans
1 (15 oz.) can diced tomatoes with garlic and
    herbs
1 cup canned corn
2 tbsp. instant minced onion or 2 tsp. onion
    powder

1/2 cup beef broth
1 tsp. sugar
2 tsp. Dijon mustard
2 tbsp. tomato paste
8 frankfurters

Combine all the ingredients except the frankfurters in a saucepan. Slowly bring to a boil. Reduce the heat and simmer for 5 minutes. Add the frankfurters, whole or sliced, and cook to heat through, about 5 minutes.

Serves 4

lamb steaks with hot slaw

see variations page 148

A hot slaw is perfect on a cool day when the thought of a cold salad doesn't appeal. A flavored oil is used to scent the lamb, but if you didn't get any as a birthday gift this year, use olive oil and a little chopped rosemary instead.

4 lamb steaks or chops, about 4–6 oz. each,
    about 1-inch thick
salt and black pepper
2 tbsp. rosemary- or other herb-flavored olive
    oil, divided

for the hot slaw
1 tsp. caraway seeds

1 medium red onion, finely sliced
2 firm Bosc pears, peeled, cored, and cut
    into wedges
1/2 red cabbage, shredded
2 medium beets, peeled and shredded
3 tbsp. red wine vinegar
1 tsp. sugar
salt and black pepper

Season the lamb steaks with salt and pepper to taste, and rub with about 1 tablespoon oil. Broil or grill for 3–4 minutes on each side, depending on how thick the meat is and how you like yours cooked. Lamb steaks are generally served when well browned on the outside and just pink in the middle. Keep warm while finishing the slaw.

Meanwhile, heat the remaining oil in a skillet and cook the caraway seeds for 30 seconds. Add the red onion and pears, and cook, stirring often, for 2 minutes. Add the cabbage and beets, and continue cooking for 5 minutes, stirring often. Pour in the red wine vinegar and sugar, and season generously with salt and black pepper.

Serves 4

italian meatballs in tomato sauce

see variations page 149

These meatballs are quick to prepare and cook, and you have the benefit of knowing they're not made with low-grade meat. Do not buy extra lean beef or the meatballs will crumble. Serve these polpette over spaghetti or with mashed potatoes.

for the meatballs
1 lb. ground beef
1/3 cup dried breadcrumbs
1/4 cup shredded Parmesan cheese
1 tbsp. minced dried onion
1 egg, lightly beaten
1 tsp. dried oregano
salt and pepper, to taste

for the sauce
2 1/2 cups tomato sauce
2 tbsp. minced dried onion
1/2 tsp. garlic powder
1 vegetable bouillon cube
1/2 cup water
salt and pepper
2 tbsp. fresh chopped basil

Preheat oven to 425°F.

Mix all the ingredients for the meatballs together in a large bowl. Shape beef mixture into 1-inch balls with dampened hands and transfer to a baking pan. Bake for about 15 minutes, or until meatballs are cooked through.

Meanwhile, in a saucepan, combine the ingredients for the sauce, except for the basil. Bring to a boil, stirring, then simmer for 5 minutes. Add the basil and pour the sauce over the cooked meatballs, then toss and return to the oven for 2 minutes.

Serves 4

sticky bbq-glazed sausages

see variations page 150

Sausages are great for quick meals, and these are cooked with a BBQ sauce for added piquancy. Serve with French fries or mashed potatoes, or in a bun.

1 lb. thick pork sausages
zest of 1 orange
juice of 1 orange
3 tbsp. honey
1 tbsp. soy sauce

1 tsp. Tabasco
1/4 tsp. ground nutmeg
1/4 tsp. ground ginger
1/4 tsp. Dijon mustard

Preheat a broiler or grill to medium.

Separate the sausages. Place all the remaining ingredients in a dish and mix well. Add the sausages and toss to coat.

Broil or grill for 10 minutes, turning the sausages frequently and basting with the glaze. The sausages should be dark and show no signs of pink inside when cooked.

Serves 4

beef & mushroom puff pie

see variations page 151

This recipe is great for cheats. By cooking the puff pastry separately, you get pie in no time, and you can use canned mushrooms if you haven't any fresh ones.

1 package ready-to-bake puff pastry
1 tsp. milk
1 tsp. sesame seeds
2 tbsp. sunflower oil
1 lb. lean ground steak
1 medium onion, finely chopped
2 tbsp. flour

1 tbsp. tomato paste
1 cup beef broth (or 1/2 cup beef broth and 1/2 cup red wine)
1 tsp. Worcestershire sauce
1 tsp. thyme
3 oz. mushrooms, sliced

Preheat the oven to 400°F. Lay the puff pastry on a lightly floured cutting board. Take a four-cup pie dish and lay on top of the pastry. Use this as a template and, using a sharp knife, cut out a pastry lid. Brush lightly with milk and sprinkle with sesame seeds. Transfer to a baking sheet lined with baking parchment; put in the refrigerator. Leave pie dish in a warm place.

Heat the oil in a deep skillet and brown the beef for 4–5 minutes, breaking it up with a wooden spoon as it cooks. Put the pastry lid in the oven and cook for 15 minutes, until golden. Add the onion to the beef and cook for 5 minutes, until soft. Stir in the flour, cook for 2 minutes, then add the remaining ingredients. Bring to a boil, then reduce the heat and simmer uncovered until the crust is cooked. Transfer the mixture to the pie dish and top with the prepared lid. Serve with fresh vegetables.

Serves 4

middle eastern spice-rubbed lamb chops

see variations page 152

Using a dry spice rub is the easiest way to impart full flavor to a piece of meat. Here a Middle Eastern spice mix is used with lamb, but it would work well with other meats or poultry, too. Serve with a couscous salad and a plate of sliced tomatoes drenched in olive oil and vinegar.

for the spice rub
1 tbsp. ground cumin
2 tsp. ground turmeric
1 tsp. paprika
1 tsp. ground coriander
1/4 tsp. garlic powder
1/2 teaspoon hot red pepper flakes
1/4 tsp. salt

4 large or 8 small lamb chops
1 tbsp. olive oil
1 lemon, quartered

Preheat the broiler or grill to high.

Combine all the ingredients for the spice rub. Brush the chops with olive oil. Press the rub into the meat on both sides using your hands.

Broil or grill the chops 7–8 minutes, turning once, for medium rare; 10–12 minutes for medium to medium well. Serve with wedges of lemon.

Serves 4

pork schnitzel

see variations page 153

Children and the young at heart love anything covered in crispy breadcrumbs, so you can be sure this will be a favorite. Serve with potato salad (page 74), hot slaw (page 136), or a warm buttered and herbed pasta.

4 5–6 oz. boneless pork cutlets or 1 1/4 lb. pork
    tenderloin sliced diagonally into 4 thin
    pieces
3/4 cup all-purpose flour
1 egg
1 tsp. lemon juice

1 cup breadcrumbs
1 tbsp. dried parsley flakes or sage
salt and pepper
sunflower oil, for frying
lemon wedges, to serve

Put the meat between two pieces of plastic wrap and pound until it is no more than 1/4-inch thick; pat dry with paper towels. Put the flour in a shallow dish. In a second shallow dish, beat the egg, then stir in the lemon juice. In a third shallow dish, combine the breadcrumbs, parsley or sage, and season generously with salt and pepper. Dip the meat first in the flour, then in the egg, and finally in the breadcrumbs, making sure to coat both sides.

In a deep skillet, heat about 1/4-inch oil to about 350°F. Add the pork and fry on each side until golden, about 4–5 minutes on each side. Serve with the lemon wedges.

Serves 4

medallions of pork with lemon & parsley

see base recipe page 131

medallions of pork with lime & cilantro
Prepare the basic recipe, adding 1 crumbled dried chile with the wine.
Replace lemon and parsley with lime and cilantro.

medallions of pork with black olive, orange & chive
Prepare the basic recipe, replacing lemon with orange and adding
1 teaspoon of orange zest. Replace parsley with chives and add 6 quartered
black olives.

chicken tenders with lemon & parsley
Prepare the basic recipe, replacing pork with 1 pound of chicken tenders.
Pound as instructed for the pork and cook in the skillet until cooked
through, 5–6 minutes.

sole with lemon & parsley butter
Prepare the basic recipe, replacing olive oil with butter. Replace pork with
4 sole fillets, seasoned with salt and pepper to taste; do not pound. Cook the
fish for about 2 minutes on each side, or until cooked through.

variations

steak with horseradish butter

see base recipe page 133

steak with garlic & chive butter
Prepare the basic recipe, omitting horseradish, mustard, and parsley. Flavor the butter with 2 minced garlic cloves and 2 tablespoons chopped fresh chives.

steak with chile-lime butter
Prepare the basic recipe, omitting horseradish, mustard, and parsley. Flavor the butter with zest of 1 lime; 1 small red chile, deseeded and finely chopped (or 1 teaspoon canned chipotle chile); and 2 tablespoons chopped fresh cilantro.

steak with piquant anchovy butter
Prepare the basic recipe, omitting horseradish, mustard, and parsley. Flavor the butter with 3 mashed anchovy fillets; 1 tablespoon each drained caper berries, chopped dill pickle, and fresh chopped parsley; 1 teaspoon each Dijon mustard and lemon juice; and 1/4 teaspoon black pepper.

steak with green peppercorn butter
Prepare the basic recipe, omitting horseradish, mustard, and parsley. Flavor the butter with 1 tablespoon green peppercorns from a jar, drained and slightly chopped; 1 tablespoon minced shallot; 1 teaspoon lemon juice; 1/2 teaspoon Dijon mustard; 2 tablespoons fresh chopped parsley; and a few drops of Worcestershire sauce.

variations

gingered beef & broccoli stir-fry

see base recipe page 134

beef & broccoli stir-fry with oyster sauce
Prepare the basic recipe, using only 2 tablespoons of soy sauce and adding 3 tablespoons of oyster sauce.

gingered chicken & broccoli stir-fry
Prepare the basic recipe, replacing the beef with 1 pound of thinly sliced chicken meat.

sichuan beef stir-fry
Prepare the basic recipe, omitting the ginger. Use only 3 tablespoons of soy sauce, and add 3 tablespoons hoisin sauce and 2–3 teaspoons of chili paste, to taste.

gingered tofu & broccoli stir-fry
Prepare the basic recipe, omitting the beef. Use 1 pound extra-firm tofu, which has been pressed, drained, and cut into 1/2-inch pieces. Stir-fry until crisp, then set aside and keep warm.

variations

instant frank & beans pot

see base recipe page 135

vegetarian sausage & beans pot
Prepare the basic recipe, replacing frankfurters with vegetarian sausages.

ham & beans pot
Prepare the basic recipe, replacing frankfurters with 12 ounces diced ham.

spicy frank & beans pot
Prepare the basic recipe, adding 1 to 2 tablespoons of Thai sweet chili sauce and a few drops of Tabasco, to taste.

frank, rice & beans pot
Prepare the basic recipe, increasing broth to 3/4 cup and adding 1 cup cooked rice with the frankfurters.

variations

lamb steak with hot slaw

see base recipe page 136

pork steak with hot slaw
Prepare the basic recipe, replacing lamb steaks with pork steaks. Increase cooking time to 6–8 minutes on each side; ensure pork is cooked through.

lamb steak with fennel slaw
Prepare the basic recipe, omitting caraway seeds. Replace the red onion, red cabbage, and beet with a sliced white onion, 2 finely sliced medium-size fennel bulbs, and a sliced carrot.

lamb steak with remoulade
Prepare the basic recipe, omitting the hot slaw. To make the remoulade, peel a 1-pound celeriac and shred into matchstick-size pieces, dropping them into a bowl containing the juice of 1/2 lemon as you chop. In another bowl, combine 2 tablespoons each of mayonnaise, heavy cream, and fresh chopped parsley with 2 teaspoons Dijon mustard. Toss with shredded celeriac; add salt and pepper to taste.

lamb steak with asian slaw
Prepare the basic recipe, omitting vinegar and sugar. Season the slaw with 1 tablespoon each soy sauce and sugar, 1/2 tablespoon balsamic vinegar, and 1 tsp. sesame oil, then season with salt and pepper to taste.

italian meatballs in tomato sauce

see base recipe page 138

swedish meatballs

Prepare the basic recipe, omitting the sauce and replacing the Worcestershire sauce and egg in the meatballs with 1/2 cup milk and 1/4 teaspoon nutmeg. When the meatballs are cooked, remove and keep warm. Drain all but 2 tablespoons fat from the pan, blend 2 tablespoons flour into the remaining fat, then slowly add 1 1/4 cups beef broth, 1 cup sour cream, and 1 tablespoon paprika, and cook over a medium heat, stirring until the sauce thickens. Proceed as directed.

meatballs with hot & sour sauce

Prepare the basic recipe, omitting the sauce. In a saucepan, combine 2 teaspoons red chili flakes, 2/3 cup corn syrup, and 1 cup apple cider vinegar. Proceed as directed.

albondigas

Prepare the basic recipe. Make the meatballs as directed, omitting the Parmesan, using 1/2 ground beef and 1/2 ground pork, and adding 1 teaspoon ground cumin. For the sauce, deseed and finely chop 2–4 medium hot red chiles, and cook in 1 tablespoon corn oil for 2–3 minutes, until soft. Proceed as directed, replacing the basil with cilantro.

variations

sticky bbq-glazed sausages

see base recipe page 139

pork kebabs in sticky glaze

Prepare the glaze following the basic recipe. Omit the sausages. Thread
1 pound cubed pork onto metal skewers (or wooden skewers soaked for
30 minutes in water). Cook as for sausages for 15–20 minutes, turning
regularly, until the pork is cooked through and lightly charred at the edges.

sausages in pineapple glaze

Prepare the basic recipe, but make the glaze from 1 cup pineapple juice,
3 tablespoons ketchup, 1 tablespoon each soy sauce and peanut oil, and
1/2 teaspoon Chinese five-spice powder.

ham steaks with sticky glaze

Prepare the glaze following the basic recipe. Replace sausages with 4 thick
ham steaks. Broil or grill, following the basic instructions, for 8–10 minutes,
until cooked through.

chicken drumsticks in sticky glaze

Prepare the glaze following the basic recipe. Replace sausages with
8 chicken drumsticks. Grill, following the basic instructions, for
10–15 minutes per side, until cooked through.

beef & mushroom puff pie

see base recipe page 140

beef & corn puff pie
Prepare the basic recipe, replacing mushrooms with 1 cup frozen or canned corn.

beef & vegetable puff pie
Prepare the basic recipe, replacing mushrooms with 1 cup frozen or canned diced mixed vegetables.

chicken & mushroom puff pie
Prepare the crust following the basic recipe. For the filling, combine 12 ounces chopped cooked chicken, 4 ounces chopped ham, 3 ounces sliced mushrooms, 1 (10-ounce) can condensed cream of chicken soup, and 1/2 teaspoon Worcestershire sauce. Heat through and cook for 5 minutes. Season to taste with pepper and top with the prepared crust.

lamb & mint puff pie
Prepare the basic recipe, replacing beef and thyme with ground lamb and 1/4 cup fresh chopped mint (4 teaspoons dried mint).

middle eastern spice–rubbed lamb chops

see base recipe page 142

mediterranean herb–rubbed lamb chops
Prepare the basic recipe, replacing the spice rub with one made using
1/2 teaspoon each of dried rosemary and oregano, and a 1/4 teaspoon each
of basil, marjoram, sage, garlic powder, salt, and black pepper.

hungarian spice–rubbed lamb chops
Prepare the basic recipe, replacing the spice rub with 1 1/2 tablespoons
sweet paprika; 1/2 tablespoon each of ground cinnamon, ground cumin, and
ground coriander; 1/2 teaspoon of oregano; and 1/4 teaspoon each of garlic
powder and salt. For more heat, add up to 1 teaspoon cayenne pepper.

french herb & garlic–rubbed lamb chops
Prepare the basic recipe, replacing the spice rub with 2 minced garlic cloves;
grated rind of 1 lemon; 1 tablespoon chopped fresh rosemary; 1 teaspoon
each chopped fresh thyme, parsley, and sage; 1/4 teaspoon salt; and a
generous pinch cayenne pepper.

bbq-rubbed lamb chops
Prepare the basic recipe, replacing the spice rub with 1 tablespoon each of
brown sugar, cumin, chili powder, mustard powder, and paprika;
1/2 teaspoon salt; and 1/4 teaspoon each garlic powder and black pepper.

variations

pork schnitzel

see base recipe page 143

pork schnitzel with sour cream sauce
Prepare the basic recipe. Once the cutlets are cooked, remove from the skillet
and keep warm. To the skillet add 3/4 cup chicken broth (or part white wine
and part broth) and use a wooden spoon to deglaze the pan, scraping all the
browned bits from its base; the mixture should reduce by one-third. Stir in
1/2 cup sour cream, 2 teaspoons fresh chopped dill (or 1/2 teaspoon dried dill),
and season with salt and pepper to taste. Heat through without boiling.

wiener schnitzel
Prepare the basic recipe, replacing pork with 4 veal cutlets (4–5 ounces each),
pounded to about 1/8-inch thick. Cook as directed, but the veal will take
2 minutes per side.

eggplant schnitzel
Prepare the basic recipe, replacing pork with 1 large eggplant. Cut the eggplant
into 3/4-inch slices. Sprinkle with salt and set aside until the salt has drawn
out the bitter liquid, at least 10 minutes. Coat in flour, egg, and breadcrumbs
as directed, and fry slowly in batches for about 3–4 minutes, until golden on
both sides.

fish

Fish is the most fantastic food for the time-pressed cook. It's extremely healthy and there are so many wonderful recipes to try — here are just a few.

Most of the fish dishes are easily adaptable to suit other fish, so buy the freshest you can or choose your favorite; simply substitute one fish steak with another meaty fish, or a flat fish such as sole with another flat fish such as flounder.

pecan-crusted salmon on spinach

see variations page 168

This is a wonderful dish, perfect for a party as you can prepare the salmon in advance and pop it into the oven when needed; for simplicity, serve with a green salad instead of spinach. The recipe works well with other fish such as halibut, tilapia, and cod.

1/3 cup finely chopped pecans
3 tbsp. dry breadcrumbs
1 tsp. grated lemon zest
2 tbsp. fresh chopped parsley or 2 tsp. dried
   parsley
4 salmon fillets, about 5 oz. each

salt and black pepper
1/4 cup mayonnaise, preferably nonfat
1/4 tsp. butter
1 lb. baby spinach, washed
whole nutmeg, grated
lemon wedges, to serve

Preheat the oven to 400°F.

In a shallow dish, combine the pecans, breadcrumbs, lemon zest, and parsley; this is most easily done in the food processor. Season each fish fillet with salt and pepper to taste. Spread mayonnaise evenly over the top of the fish, then press down into the pecan mixture, coating the fish with crumbs. Put the fish into a lightly buttered baking pan. Bake for 12–15 minutes, until the fish is browned and the fish flakes easily with a fork.

Meanwhile, steam the spinach over a pan of boiling water for about 2 minutes, until just cooked; drain. Arrange the spinach in the center of each plate, grate over a little nutmeg, top with the fish, and serve with lemon wedges.

Serves 4

halibut with fresh tomato salsa

see variations page 169

Halibut is a delicious firm, meaty fish, but it is endangered in the Atlantic, so look for North Pacific or line-caught halibut. If overcooked, halibut may dry out, so be sure to serve as soon as it is ready.

for the salsa
1 lb. ripe, well-flavored tomatoes
2 tbsp. olive oil
1 small red onion, finely chopped
1 garlic clove, minced
1–2 jalapeño chiles, deseeded and finely
    chopped
1/4 cup fresh chopped cilantro
1 tbsp. lime juice

1/2 tsp. sugar
salt and black pepper

1/4 cup all-purpose flour
4 halibut steaks, 1-inch thick
salt and pepper
juice of 1 lemon
2 tbsp. olive oil

To make the salsa, pour boiling water over the tomatoes, remove them after 30 seconds, then peel with a sharp knife. Cut into quarters, scoop out the seeds, then roughly chop. Add the remaining salsa ingredients, adjusting the quantities to taste.

Put the flour on a plate in an even layer. Pat the fish dry with paper towels, season the fish with salt and pepper to taste, then dip into the flour on both sides to lightly coat. Heat the olive oil in a skillet and cook the fish for about 4–5 minutes on each side. Serve accompanied by the salsa.

Serves 4

singapore noodles

see variations page 170

This dish uses rice vermicelli noodles, so it is gluten-free. However, it does combine precooked meat and seafood. If you don't like meat, double up on the shrimp or use a combination of shrimp and mussels. Don't be put off by the long list of ingredients — it's a very easy dish to prepare.

8 oz. rice vermicelli
1/4 cup sunflower oil, divided
2 eggs, lightly beaten
3 tbsp. soy sauce
1 chicken bouillon cube, crumbled
1 tsp. medium curry powder
1/2 tsp. ground ginger
1 tsp. sesame oil
pinch sugar

3 oz. snow peas
4 green onions, thinly sliced
1/2 green bell pepper, thinly sliced
1/2 red bell pepper, thinly sliced
6 oz. cooked beef, pork, or chicken, cut into
    strips
6 oz. small shrimp
3 oz. bean sprouts

Cook the vermicelli in boiling water for 1 minute, drain, and leave in the covered pan to finish cooking. After 3 minutes, remove the lid and separate the strands with a fork. Put the lid back on and keep in a warm place.

Meanwhile, heat 1 tablespoon sunflower oil in a skillet and add the beaten eggs. Cook like an omelet until set. Remove from the pan and roll up, then cut into strips. Keep warm with the vermicelli.

In a bowl, mix 1 tablespoon sunflower oil, soy sauce, crumbled bouillon cube, curry powder, ground ginger, sesame oil, and sugar. Set aside.

Heat the remaining oil in a large wok, then add the snow peas and stir-fry for 1 minute, add the green onions and bell peppers, and stir-fry for another minute. Add the beef, pork, or chicken and the shrimp, and stir-fry for 2 minutes. Add the vermicelli and egg along with the bean sprouts and the soy sauce mixture, and stir-fry to heat through, tossing to mix the ingredients evenly.

Serves 4

monkfish with citrus tapenade

see variations page 171

Tapenade is a delicious black olive paste that hails from southern France. All this zingy fish dish needs as an accompaniment is a dish of new potatoes and a bowl of lightly dressed mixed salad leaves.

4 monkfish fillets, skinned, about 6 oz. each
1/4 cup all-purpose flour
salt and black pepper, to taste
2 tsp. butter
1 tsp. orange zest

for the citrus tapenade
3/4 cup tapenade from a jar
2 tbsp. orange juice
1 tsp. orange zest
1 tbsp. lemon juice
1/4 tsp. lemon zest
1 tbsp. lime juice
1/4 tsp. lime zest
pinch sugar

Preheat broiler to medium high. Put the flour on a plate in an even layer. Pat the fish dry with paper towels, season the fish with salt and pepper, then dip into the flour on both sides to lightly coat. Lay fillets on a lightly oiled broiler pan and dot them with butter. Sprinkle 1 teaspoon orange zest on the fillets. Broil about 4–5 minutes on each side, depending on the thickness of the fish, or until fish flakes easily.

Meanwhile, mix the tapenade with the citrus juices and zests. Add sugar and salt and black pepper to taste. Serve fish accompanied by the tapenade.

Serves 4

crab cakes with caribbean salsa

see variations page 172

A great favorite with everyone, these crab cakes freeze well before cooking, so double up the recipe and put some away for another day.

1 lb. crabmeat, preferably fresh or frozen and
   thawed
1 garlic clove, minced
1/2 red medium bell pepper, finely chopped
2 green onions, finely chopped
2 tbsp. chopped fresh parsley
2 tbsp. mayonnaise
1 tbsp. Dijon mustard
zest of 1 lemon
1/2 tsp. paprika
1/2 tsp. salt
black pepper
2 eggs, lightly beaten

1 cup breadcrumbs, divided
2–4 tbsp. sweet butter

for the caribbean salsa
1 (10-oz.) can tropical fruit salad, drained
6 oz. strawberries, chopped
3 tbsp. finely chopped red onion
3 tbsp. finely chopped red bell pepper
3 tbsp. chopped fresh cilantro
1 tbsp. finely chopped deseeded jalapeño chile
juice of 1/2 lime
salt and pepper, to taste

In a bowl, combine the crabmeat, garlic, bell pepper, green onions, parsley, mayonnaise, mustard, lemon zest, paprika, salt, and several grindings of black pepper. Stir in the eggs, then mix in half of the breadcrumbs using clean hands or a wooden spoon.

Using a 1/4 measuring cup as a scoop, form approximately 12 crab cakes. Put the remaining breadcrumbs in a shallow dish. Dredge the crab cakes in breadcrumbs.

Heat 2 tablespoons butter in a skillet and cook half of the crab cakes over medium heat for 3–4 minutes each side, or until golden brown. Repeat with the remaining crab cakes, adding more butter to the skillet as needed.

While the crab cakes are cooking, combine all the ingredients for the salsa and serve on the side with the cooked crab cakes.

Makes 12 crab cakes

fish in foil

see variations page 173

This is a fantastic way to cook fish. Wrapping in packets means that, in effect, the food is steamed in its own moisture, retaining all its flavor and goodness. If you are cooking in your oven rather than on an outside grill, you can use baking parchment in place of foil, but be sure to wrap the edges tightly together.

4 6-oz. fillets of fish (cod, haddock, tilapia,
   tuna, or salmon)
2 tbsp. olive oil
salt and pepper
8 lemon slices
1 red bell pepper, sliced

1 zucchini, sliced
1 small red onion, sliced
4 small tomatoes, quartered
8 small mushrooms, halved
1/4 cup chopped fresh parsley
1/4 cup lemon juice or white wine

Preheat the barbecue or the oven to 400°F. Brush the fish with olive oil, and season with salt and pepper to taste. Top with lemon slices and set aside.

Cut 4 pieces of aluminum foil, large enough to envelop the fish fillets. Put the remaining ingredients in the center of each piece of foil, dividing equally. Top with the fish. Seal the packets very tightly.

Cook the packages on the barbecue or in the oven for 15–20 minutes. To check for doneness, pry open one of the packets with a fork and check that the fish is cooked through. Make a slit in the foil to allow steam to escape before opening packets.

Serves 4

baked breaded scallops

see variations page 174

These tasty scallops make a lovely light meal accompanied by a mango salsa, such as the one on page 169, or an avocado salad. They are every bit as good as their deep-fried cousins, but much lower in fat.

1 cup fresh breadcrumbs or crispbread
    ground to crumbs
1/4 cup olive oil
1/4 cup shredded Parmesan cheese
1 tbsp. chopped fresh parsley

zest of 1 lemon
1/4 teaspoon garlic powder
pinch cayenne pepper
salt and pepper, to taste
24 prepared scallops

Preheat oven to 400°F. In a bowl, mix together the breadcrumbs, oil, Parmesan, parsley, lemon zest, garlic powder, and cayenne pepper, with salt and pepper to taste.

Dry the scallops on paper towels, then toss with the breadcrumb mixture. Put in an ovenproof serving dish and cook for 9–12 minutes, until the scallops are opaque and the crust golden brown; do not overcook as they will become chewy and tough.

Serves 3–4

simple sole meunière

see variations page 175

Sole is a very delicate flat fish that cooks in no time at all. It is classically served in this butter sauce with new potatoes and a steamed green vegetable or a zucchini ratatouille.

1/4 cup flour
4 lemon sole fillets, skinned, 3–4 oz. each
salt and black pepper
1/3 stick butter, divided

1 tsp. lemon zest
1/4 cup lemon juice
1 tbsp. fresh chopped parsley

Put the flour on a plate in an even layer. Pat the fish dry with paper towels, season with salt and pepper to taste, then dip into the flour on both sides to lightly coat.

The fish is cooked in two batches. Heat 1/2 of the butter in a skillet, add the fish skin side down and cook over medium-low heat for 2 minutes, carefully turning the fish over with a spatula. Cook for 1 minute, then add 1/2 of the lemon zest and juice and cook for 1 additional minute, or until the fish is golden. Put the fish on plates, pour the sauce on top, and keep warm. Wipe the skillet with a paper towel and repeat with the second batch of fish. Serve sprinkled with the fresh parsley.

Serves 4

variations

pecan-crusted salmon on spinach

see base recipe page 155

hazelnut-crusted salmon
Prepare the basic recipe, replacing pecans with finely chopped hazelnuts.

pan-fried pecan-crusted fish
Prepare the basic recipe, but spread mayonnaise on both sides of the fish and coat the fish on both sides with a thin layer of the breadcrumb mixture. Heat 2 tablespoons sunflower oil in a skillet large enough to hold all of the fish. Cook over medium-low heat for 3–4 minutes on each side, until browned and fish flakes easily with a fork. Note: This variation works better with thin to medium rather than thick fish fillets.

pecan-crusted pork
Prepare the basic recipe, replacing salmon with 4 pork chops. Replace the mayonnaise with honey-mustard salad dressing. Bake for 18–25 minutes, depending on the thickness of the chops.

pine nut- & pesto-crusted fish
Prepare the basic recipe, replacing the pecans, breadcrumbs, lemon zest, and parsley with 1/3 cup chopped pine nuts, 2 tablespoons shredded Parmesan cheese, 1 teaspoon pesto, and 1/4 teaspoon garlic powder.

halibut with fresh tomato salsa

see base recipe page 157

halibut with tomato–olive salsa
Prepare the basic recipe, replacing the chiles and cilantro with 10 pitted and finely chopped kalamata olives and 2 tablespoons of finely shredded basil.

halibut with mango salsa
Prepare the basic recipe, replacing the tomatoes and garlic with the rough chopped flesh of 1 large mango and 1/4 finely chopped red bell pepper. Increase the lime juice to 2 tablespoons.

halibut with salsa verde
Prepare the basic recipe, omitting the salsa. In a food processor, drop through the tube 5 garlic cloves to mince. Add 2 cups each fresh parsley and fresh cilantro, and process until very fine. Transfer to a bowl and mix with the juice of 2 lemons, 1/4 cup each olive oil and apple cider vinegar, and salt and pepper to taste.

tuna with fresh tomato salsa
Prepare the basic recipe, replacing the halibut with four 6-ounce tuna steaks. Cook for 2 minutes on each side for medium and 3–4 minutes for well done.

singapore noodles

see base recipe page 158

singapore stir-fry with rice
Prepare the basic recipe, omitting the vermicelli. Cook 1 1/4 cups of basmati or long grain rice according to the package directions; drain and toss with the egg. Sprinkle with 1 teaspoon sesame oil and mix. Serve the stir-fried mixture over the rice.

vegetarian singapore noodles
Prepare the basic recipe, replacing the meat and shrimp with a 12-ounce package of pressed, drained, extra-firm tofu, diced.

fiery singapore noodles
Prepare the basic recipe, adding 1 deseeded and sliced red chile to the stir-fry with the bell peppers, and serving another sprinkled on the top of the finished dish. Serve with lime wedges.

sweet & spicy noodles
Prepare the basic recipe, replacing the sauce with pineapple glaze, page 150.

variations

monkfish with citrus tapenade

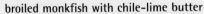

see base recipe page 161

broiled monkfish with chile-lime butter
Prepare the basic recipe, omitting the tapenade and serving with a wedge of chile-lime butter (see page 145).

broiled monkfish taco
Prepare the basic recipe, omitting the tapenade. Replace orange with lime zest, and add a pinch of chili flakes per fillet. Flake the cooked fish and serve in a taco shell with a selection of: thinly sliced red onion, bell peppers, tomatoes, shredded lettuce or white cabbage, chopped cilantro, chili sauce or sour cream.

broiled monkfish with caper & lemon sauce
Prepare the basic recipe, omitting the tapenade. Replace orange with lemon zest. For the sauce, heat through 1/3 cup butter or olive oil, 1 minced garlic clove, 3 mashed anchovy fillets, grated zest and juice of 1 lemon, 2 tablespoons chopped capers, 1 tablespoon chopped fresh parsley, and black pepper to taste.

chicken with citrus tapenade
Replace the monkfish with chicken cooked according to the directions on page 105, but omitting lemon and thyme. Serve with the tapenade prepared as for the basic recipe.

variations

crab cakes with caribbean salsa

see base recipe page 162

ginger crab cakes
Prepare the basic recipe, adding to the crabmeat 1-inch fresh ginger, peeled and minced, and 1/4 teaspoon Tabasco sauce.

crab & shrimp cakes
Prepare the basic recipe, using only 8 ounces crabmeat and 8 ounces of raw, prepared shrimp, chopped into small pieces.

fish cakes
Prepare the basic recipe, replacing crabmeat with cooked and flaked white fish, such as cod or tilapia, or salmon. Add a few finely chopped shrimp, if desired.

crab cake canapés
Prepare the basic recipe, halving the size of the crab cakes. Lightly mash the salsa and put 1/2 teaspoon on top of each crab cake. Garnish with a tiny sprig of parsley.

variations

fish in foil

see base recipe page 164

fish with fennel & orange in foil
Prepare the basic recipe for cooking the fish. For the vegetable base, blanch
a large finely sliced fennel bulb for 2 minutes. Divide among the 4 packets
with 1 small sliced white onion, 1/4 cup parsley, and the zest and chopped
flesh of the orange. Top the fish with orange slices instead of lemon slices.

fish & herbed tomatoes in foil
Prepare the basic recipe for cooking the fish. For the vegetable base, divide
1 (15-ounce) can drained chopped tomatoes among the 4 packets, and also
divide 1/4 cup chopped sundried tomatoes, 1 small sliced red onion, 1/4 cup
basil, 1/4 cup white wine or lemon juice, and salt and pepper to taste.

fish with mushrooms, garlic & ginger in foil
Prepare the basic recipe for cooking the fish. For the vegetable base, divide
2 ounces each of sliced oyster and cremini mushrooms among the 4 packets.
In addition, divide up 1 minced garlic clove; 1-inch fresh ginger, peeled and
minced; 1/4 cup tamari sauce; and 1 teaspoon sesame oil.

shrimp in foil
Prepare the basic recipe, replacing fish with 1 1/2 pounds of large shelled
and deveined shrimp with tails left on. Cook for about 8–10 minutes.

variations

baked breaded scallops

see base recipe page 165

breaded fish sticks
Prepare the basic recipe for the breadcrumb mixture. Omit scallops. Preheat oven to 400°F. Cut about 1 pound firm white fish fillets into 3/4-inch-thick strips. Put 1/4 cup flour on a plate. Season the fish with salt and pepper to taste, then dip into the flour on both sides. Beat 1 egg in a shallow bowl with 2 tablespoons water, dip the fish fingers in the egg, then in the breadcrumb mixture. Put on a baking sheet. Bake for about 15 minutes.

herb breaded scallops
Prepare the basic recipe, adding 1/4 cup each of chopped dill and chopped chives to the breadcrumb mixture.

creole breaded scallops
Prepare the basic recipe but, for the breadcrumb mixture, omit Parmesan and add 3 teaspoons Creole spice blend and 1 teaspoon Tabasco sauce.

breaded scallops with garlic cream dip
Prepare the basic recipe, adding 1 minced garlic clove to the breadcrumb mixture. Put 4 minced garlic cloves in a small saucepan with 1/2 cup white wine, bring to simmer, and cook for about 2 minutes. Stir in 1/2 cup heavy cream, heat through, and add salt and pepper to taste. Serve as a warm dip.

simple sole meunière

see base recipe page 166

sole with lemon & caper butter
Prepare the basic recipe, adding 1 tablespoon of capers per batch of fish to the lemon–butter sauce.

reduced-fat sole meunière
Prepare the basic recipe, replacing butter with a butter substitute. Alternatively, use 1 1/2 tablespoons each of butter and olive oil per batch of fish.

sole with garlic & paprika
Prepare the basic recipe, replacing the pepper with paprika to season the fish. Add 1/2 teaspoon minced garlic to the foaming butter in the skillet.

broiled lemon sole
Preheat the broiler. Line the broiler pan with aluminum foil. When preparing the fish, omit the flouring process. Lay the seasoned fish skin side up in the pan. Melt 1/4 cup butter and add 1 teaspoon lemon rind. Brush over the fish. Broil for 2–3 minutes, turn with a spatula, and baste with the melted butter; repeat broiling time. Serve drizzled with 2 tablespoons lemon juice and 1 tablespoon chopped parsley. Note: This method works for other flat fish, too.

pasta

Pasta is one of the most versatile pantry items ever.

Almost any sauce can be tossed with it, but many

of us love the tomato and creamy cheese sauces.

The recipes here are all quick to make and are

prepared with a minimum of fuss.

spaghetti carbonara

see variations page 190

The lovely, creamy richness is offset by the salty bacon in this classic Italian recipe. As the egg is barely cooked, this dish is best avoided by pregnant women and anyone who is immune-suppressed.

salt
12 oz. spaghetti
1 tbsp. olive oil
8 oz. pancetta, smoked bacon, or air-dried ham
4 eggs

1/2 cup half and half
1/2 cup shredded Parmesan or pecorino cheese, divided
black pepper

Set a large saucepan of slightly salted water to boil, add the spaghetti and the olive oil, and return to a boil. Cook for about 10 minutes, or according to the package directions, until just cooked (al dente).

Meanwhile, remove any rind from the pancetta or bacon and slice. Cook in a dry skillet until crisp (if using air-dried ham, omit this step). In a bowl, beat the eggs with the half and half, mix in two-thirds of the cheese, and season with plenty of black pepper to taste.

When the spaghetti is cooked, drain thoroughly, then quickly return to the saucepan and add the egg mixture and the ham, as well as any pan fat. Working quickly, toss the spaghetti in the sauce so that the eggs cook briefly on contact with the hot spaghetti. Serve at once sprinkled with the remaining cheese.

Serves 4

fettuccini with blue cheese & tomatoes

see variations page 191

This piquant dish is a perfect, quick after-work meal, and a good way to use up any blue cheese lurking in the refrigerator. Serve with a green salad and chilled white wine.

salt
14 oz. fettuccini
2 tbsp. olive oil, divided
1 medium onion, peeled and chopped
1 garlic clove, minced
8 oz. Gorgonzola, Stilton, or other blue cheese, crumbled

1/4 cup heavy cream or Greek-style yogurt
4 oz. grape tomatoes, halved
2 tbsp. chopped fresh sage or parsley
black pepper
shredded Parmesan cheese, to serve

Set a large saucepan of slightly salted water to boil, add the fettuccini and 1 tablespoon olive oil, and return to a boil. Cook for about 8 minutes, or according to the package directions, until just cooked (al dente). Drain the pasta, but reserve 1/4 cup of cooking water.

Meanwhile, heat 1 tablespoon olive oil in a saucepan, add the onion, and cook over medium heat for 5 minutes until soft. Add the garlic and cook for an additional 2 minutes. Pour the 1/4 cup of cooking water over the fried onion, stir in the crumbled cheese, and leave over low heat to melt slightly. Stir in the cream or yogurt and the tomatoes; heat through without boiling.

Add the pasta to the pan along with the sage or parsley, and toss well together. Season generously with black pepper to taste, and sprinkle some grated Parmesan on top to serve.
Serves 4

fusilli with chorizo

see variations page 192

This is a spicy, rich sauce that can be made in advance. If you haven't got fusilli, then choose another substantial pasta, such as penne or spirali.

salt
8 oz. fully cooked spicy chorizo
1 medium red onion, chopped
1 bay leaf
1 tbsp. fresh chopped rosemary (1 tsp. dried)
1 1/4 cup red wine or chicken broth
1 1/2 (15-oz.) cans chopped tomatoes

1 tbsp. tomato paste
1 tsp. chili flakes
12 oz. fusilli
1 tbsp. oil
1/4 cup heavy cream or sour cream
2 tbsp. shredded Parmesan cheese

Set a large saucepan of slightly salted water to boil.

Remove the casings from the chorizo and crumble. Put in a skillet and fry over medium-high heat until lightly browned. Remove the chorizo from the pan with a slotted spoon and keep warm. Remove all but 1 tablespoon of the chorizo fat from the pan and add the onion, bay leaf, and rosemary; cook for 5 minutes, until soft. Pour in the wine or broth, and boil for 2 minutes while deglazing the pan with a wooden spoon. Add the tomatoes, tomato paste, and chili flakes, and season with a little salt to taste. Bring to a boil, then reduce the heat, cover, and simmer while the pasta is cooking.

Add the fusilli and oil to the boiling water, and return to a boil. Cook for about 10 minutes, or according to the package directions, until just cooked (al dente); drain.

Stir the heavy cream or sour cream into the sauce, and adjust the seasoning to taste. Serve over the pasta sprinkled with Parmesan.

Serves 3

farfalle with salmon & broccoli

see variations page 193

This dish looks so pretty and is great for casual entertaining. Look for fresh farfalle instead of dried for an authentic touch.

salt
8 oz. broccoli florets, cut into small pieces
12 oz. farfalle
1 tbsp. olive oil
2 tbsp. butter

8 oz. leeks, sliced
1/2 cup sour cream or crème fraîche
8 oz. smoked salmon pieces
2 tbsp. chopped fresh dill
black pepper

Set a large saucepan of slightly salted water to boil, add the broccoli, and blanch for 2 minutes. Remove the broccoli from the water, leaving the water boiling. Refresh the broccoli under cold water and set aside. Add the farfalle and the olive oil to the boiling water, and cook for about 10 minutes, or according to the package directions. About 5 minutes before the pasta is cooked, add the broccoli.

Meanwhile, melt the butter in a skillet, add the leeks, and cook for about 4 minutes, until soft.

Drain the pasta and broccoli, return to the pan, then stir in the leeks and sour cream or crème fraîche. Heat through without boiling, remove from the heat and stir in the salmon and dill, then season with black pepper to taste.

Serves 4

pasta norma

see variations page 194

A dish full of sun-drenched Sicilian flavor. To get the best out of the dish, the eggplant should be a deep golden color and silky smooth inside. Fresh basil is also a must.

1 medium eggplant
1/4 cup olive oil, divided
2 garlic cloves, minced
salt
6 oz. spaghetti
1/4 cup red wine
1 (15-oz.) can tomato sauce

1 tsp. balsamic vinegar
1 tsp. sugar
1/2 tbsp. fresh chopped oregano or 1 tsp. dried
    oregano
black pepper
1/4 cup freshly chopped basil
1/4 cup shredded Parmesan cheese, to serve

Cut the eggplant in half and scoop out the seeded center. Cut into pieces about 1 inch long and 1/2 inch wide. Heat 3 tablespoons olive oil in a large skillet or wok. Add the eggplant and cook over medium-high heat, tossing regularly to coat all of the surfaces with oil. Fry until golden and soft, adding the garlic about 2 minutes before the eggplant is cooked.

Set a large saucepan of slightly salted water to boil, add the spaghetti and 1 tablespoon olive oil, and return to a boil. Cook for about 10 minutes, or according to the package directions, until just cooked (al dente). Drain the pasta, but reserve 1/4 cup of cooking water.

While the pasta is cooking, pour the red wine into the skillet with the eggplant and bring to a boil, then add the tomato sauce, vinegar, sugar, oregano, and salt and pepper to taste. Reduce the heat and simmer for 10 minutes. Stir in the basil, adding a little cooking liquid to thin the sauce slightly if too thick. Serve over the spaghetti, garnished with Parmesan.

Serves 2

pasta primavera

see variations page 195

The wonderful produce available in supermarkets has made the preparation of fresh vegetables possible in this "spring pasta." If pressed for time, buy your peas shelled, your beans sliced, and your spinach washed. Sometimes these items come packaged together, so mix and match, making the best of what you find.

salt	3 green onions, sliced
12 oz. tagliatelle	zest and juice of 1/2 lemon
3 tbsp. olive oil, divided	2 tbsp. fresh chopped mint
4 oz. baby carrots, cut to 1/4-in. thick	2 tbsp. fresh chopped dill or tarragon
4 oz. fine asparagus	2 tbsp. fresh chopped parsley
4 oz. ready shelled peas	black pepper
4 oz. baby spinach leaves	4 oz. soft goat cheese, crumbled

Set a large saucepan of slightly salted water to boil, add the tagliatelle and 1 tablespoon olive oil, and return to a boil. Cook for about 10 minutes, or according to the directions on the package.

Place a steamer or heatproof sieve over the pan of pasta. Add the vegetables and cover to steam. The carrots will take about 6 minutes; the asparagus and peas, 4 minutes; and the spinach and green onions, 2 minutes. Drain the pasta when just cooked (al dente), reserving 1/4 cup cooking liquid.

Return the pasta to the saucepan. Add the steamed vegetables, a little of the cooking water to loosen, the lemon zest and juice, and the fresh herbs. Season with salt and pepper to taste. Serve drizzled with the remaining olive oil and topped with crumbled goat cheese.
Serves 4

gnocchi with spinach & walnuts

see variations page 196

Gnocchi is fine and filling, and great for a near-instant supper. As it comes vacuum packed, it has a long shelf life and is a handy standby; it also freezes well.

1 lb. gnocchi	2 garlic cloves, minced
2 tbsp. sweet butter	10 oz. fresh baby spinach
1 tbsp. olive oil	salt and pepper
1/4 cup walnut pieces	1/4 cup shredded Parmesan cheese

Cook the gnocchi in a saucepan of boiling water for 2 minutes, or according to package directions. Drain, reserving 1/4 cup cooking liquid, and keep warm.

Meanwhile, heat the butter and olive oil in a large skillet, add the walnuts and cook, stirring occasionally, for 2 minutes. Add the minced garlic and cook for a further 2 minutes; the walnuts should be golden. Add the gnocchi, a little cooking water to loosen, and the spinach. Cook, stirring, until the spinach wilts. Season with salt and pepper to taste, and sprinkle with Parmesan.

Serves 4

tuna supper

see variations page 197

Comfort food at its most homey, and a winner with kids and hungry adults alike. Substituting reduced-fat milk and cheese keeps the fat and calorie count lower. A small tomato and red onion salad on the side would be a perfect match.

salt
12 oz. penne or macaroni
4 tbsp. olive oil, divided
2 1/2 cups milk
3 tbsp. all-purpose flour, sifted
pinch cayenne pepper
2 oz. sharp cheddar cheese, shredded

1 tsp. Dijon mustard
1 tsp. Worcestershire sauce
1/2 cup frozen or canned corn
1/2 cup frozen peas
2 (6-oz.) cans chunk tuna, in water, drained
black pepper
2 tbsp. fresh chopped parsley, to garnish

Set a large saucepan of slightly salted water to boil. Add the penne or macaroni and 1 tablespoon oil to the boiling water, and return to a boil. Cook for about 12 minutes, or according to the package directions, until just cooked (al dente); drain.

In a medium saucepan, put the milk, remaining olive oil, flour, and cayenne pepper. Slowly bring to a boil, stirring constantly with a balloon whisk. The sauce will thicken as it boils. Add the cheese, mustard, Worcestershire sauce, corn, peas, and tuna. Season with salt and pepper to taste, and cook for 5 minutes, until the corn and peas are heated through.

Return the pasta to the pan and toss with the sauce. Serve garnished with parsley.

Serves 4

variations

spaghetti carbonara

see base recipe page 177

spaghetti carbonara with smoked salmon
Prepare the basic recipe, replacing pancetta with smoked salmon bits. Do not precook the salmon.

spaghetti carbonara with french beans
Prepare the basic recipe. Steam 8 ounces French beans in a steamer or in a sieve over the cooking spaghetti, about 8 minutes. The beans should then be added to the cooked pasta. Omit the pancetta for a vegetarian option.

spaghetti carbonara with walnuts
Prepare the basic recipe, adding 1/2 cup chopped walnuts to the spaghetti with the cooked pancetta. Omit the pancetta for a vegetarian option.

spaghetti carbonara with spinach
Prepare the basic recipe. When the bacon is cooked, remove and add 2 cups of baby spinach leaves to the bacon fat; stir-fry for 2 minutes until tender. Add to the pasta with the bacon.

variations

fettuccine with blue cheese & tomatoes

see base recipe page 179

fettuccini with blue cheese & walnuts
Prepare the basic recipe, replacing the tomatoes with 3/4 cup chopped walnuts.

fettuccini with blue cheese & spinach
Prepare the basic recipe. When the pasta is just about done, add 8 ounces baby spinach leaves; stir. As soon as the spinach wilts completely (less than 1 minute), drain quickly and proceed as directed.

fettuccini with blue cheese & artichoke sauce
Prepare the basic recipe, replacing the tomatoes with 1 (14-ounce) can water-packed artichoke hearts, rinsed, drained, and chopped.

fettuccini with blue cheese, bacon & tomatoes
Prepare the basic recipe, cooking 3 strips of chopped bacon in with the onions.

variations

fusilli with chorizo

see base recipe page 180

lite fusilli with chorizo
Prepare the basic recipe, cooking the sausage slowly to extract as much of
the fat as possible. Replace the heavy cream with soy-based cream to cut
down on fat.

extra spicy fusilli with chorizo
Prepare the basic recipe, omitting the dried chiles and adding 2 deseeded
and chopped chiles or 2 tablespoons canned chopped chipotles to the onion
halfway through cooking.

rice with chorizo & corn
Prepare the basic recipe, adding 1 cup canned or frozen corn to the tomato
sauce. Serve over rice.

fusilli with sausage & bacon sauce
Prepare the basic recipe, replacing the chorizo with regular sausage and
cooking with 3 chopped strips of smoked bacon.

variations

farfalle with salmon & broccoli

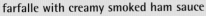

see base recipe page 182

farfalle with creamy smoked ham sauce

Prepare the basic recipe, replacing the salmon and dill with chopped smoked ham and dried sage.

farfalle with creamy seafood sauce

Prepare the basic recipe, using 8 ounces mixed seafood such as shrimp, clams, mussels, or squid. Once the leeks are cooked, remove from the pan and keep warm. Add the seafood plus another tablespoon of butter, and cook for 3–5 minutes, until cooked through. Proceed as for basic recipe.

farfalle with creamy salmon & pea sauce

Prepare the basic recipe, replacing the broccoli with 1 cup frozen peas. Add peas to the pasta water 3 minutes before the pasta is cooked.

farfalle with creamy mushroom sauce

Prepare the basic recipe, omitting the salmon and broccoli. Cook 4 ounces sliced cremini mushrooms in 1/2 cup white wine until the liquid is reduced by half and the mushrooms are tender. Add this mixture to the pasta with the cream. Fresh sage or tarragon can also be used in place of the dill.

variations

pasta norma

see base recipe page 183

pasta with zucchini & tomatoes
Prepare the basic recipe, replacing the eggplant with 2 medium zucchini. Cut zucchini into 1/4-inch slices to cook, then add the other ingredients, including the tomato sauce, as directed.

paste norma with ricotta
Prepare the basic recipe, replacing the Parmesan cheese with 8 ounces fresh ricotta cheese.

even quicker pasta norma
Prepare the basic recipe, using 1 (10-ounce) jar of charbroiled eggplant antipasto slices. Reduce the olive oil to 2 tablespoons and heat the eggplant slices through. Proceed as directed.

pasta caponata
Prepare the basic recipe. With the tomatoes add 8 pitted black olives, 2 tablespoons capers, 1 tablespoon currants, and 1/4 green bell pepper, diced. Increase the balsamic vinegar to 1 tablespoon. Use only 2 tablespoons basil; parsley can be substituted.

variations

pasta primavera

see base recipe page 185

pasta with creamy vegetables
Prepare the basic recipe, adding 2/3 cup heavy cream, crème fraîche, Greek-style yogurt, or soy cream to the steamed vegetables and pasta, and reducing the lemon juice to 1 tablespoon. Do not drizzle the finished dish with olive oil.

pasta with frozen vegetables
Prepare the basic recipe, replacing the fresh vegetables and 4 ounces frozen spinach with 1 (10-ounce) package baby vegetable medley. Steam in the bag, or cook according to package directions. Some varieties are pre-seasoned with herbs, in which case reduce the quantity of fresh herbs by half.

pasta primavera salad bowl
Prepare the basic recipe, replacing the tagliatelle with pasta shells or farfalle. Do not cook the green onions. Once cooked, plunge the vegetables in cold water to quickly chill and refresh; allow pasta to cool. Combine the pasta, vegetables, green onions, and the remaining ingredients, and toss to mix.

pasta primavera with shrimp
Prepare the basic recipe. Cook 12–16 peeled and deveined shrimp in 1 tablespoon olive oil in a skillet until they turn opaque, 3–4 minutes. Toss in with the vegetables and pasta.

variations

gnocchi with spinach & walnuts

see base recipe page 186

gnocchi with pesto & walnuts
Prepare the gnocchi as for basic recipe, omitting the spinach. For the pesto, blend the walnuts and garlic in a food processor. Melt and add the butter plus 4 tablespoons olive oil, 1 cup fresh basil leaves, and 1/2 cup Parmesan cheese; pulse until blended. Pour 2 tablespoons gnocchi cooking liquid plus 2 tablespoons half and half into the drained gnocchi, then stir in the pesto. Season with salt and pepper to taste.

gnocchi with tomato–spinach sauce
Prepare the gnocchi as for basic recipe, omitting the walnuts. Serve with a tomato sauce (see introduction page 15) and garnish with Parmesan cheese.

gnocchi with brown butter & sage
Prepare the gnocchi as for basic recipe, omitting the spinach and olive oil. Increase the butter to 2/3 stick. With the walnuts add about 20 small sage leaves, and cook until the sage has crisped and the butter is turning a golden brown color. Proceed as directed.

gnocchi with creamy spinach-walnut sauce
Follow the basic recipe, adding 1/2 cup heavy cream just as the spinach has wilted. Bring to a boil and proceed as directed.

tuna supper

see base recipe page 189

tuna with crisp cheese topping
Prepare the basic recipe. Combine the pasta and sauce in a shallow heatproof dish. Combine 1 cup soft breadcrumbs with 1/4 cup shredded cheddar cheese and 2 tablespoons olive oil. Sprinkle over the pasta and put under a hot broiler until crisp and golden.

tuna & cream cheese corn bake
Prepare the pasta as directed, omitting the milk, flour, and 3 tablespoons olive oil. For the sauce, heat 8 ounces low-fat cream cheese with 1 1/2 cups chicken broth. Add the remaining ingredients and proceed as directed. Using reduced-fat cheese keeps the fat and calorie count lower.

tuna with tomato & corn
Prepare the pasta as directed, omitting the milk, flour, 3 tablespoons olive oil, and mustard. Make a tomato sauce (see introduction page 15) or use a purchased tomato pasta sauce. Add remaining ingredients; proceed as directed.

mediterranean-style tuna supper
Prepare the tuna with tomato & corn recipe above, omitting the corn. Add 1 cup diced bell peppers, 1/2 cup diced onion, and 1/2 cup diced black olives to the tomato sauce; proceed as directed.

vegetarian

Vegetarian dishes aren't just for vegetarians — they make great, healthy meals for the whole family. These recipes range from those based on the bright flavors of fresh vegetables to those exploiting the great versatility of eggs, and to others based on the earthy tastes of beans and lentils.

Don't forget that there are also loads of vegetarian options in the variations section of other chapters.

peperonata with crispy polenta

see variations page 217

Peperonata is a zingy, tasty, and versatile dish that works well hot or at room temperature. Here it is teamed up with that fantastic pantry standby: ready-to-serve polenta.

3 tbsp. olive oil
1 large white onion, thinly sliced
1 garlic clove, thinly sliced
1 red bell pepper, deseeded and sliced into strips
1 yellow bell pepper, deseeded and sliced into strips

pinch of dried chili flakes
1 (15 oz.) can chopped tomatoes
1/4 tsp. sugar
salt and black pepper
1 (1 lb.) package ready-made polenta
2 tbsp. butter or olive oil

Heat the oil in a shallow saucepan or skillet, add the onion, and cook over a moderate heat for 5 minutes, until soft. Add the garlic, bell peppers, and chili flakes; cook, stirring frequently, for 3–4 minutes until the peppers begin to soften. Add the tomatoes and sugar, then season to taste with salt and pepper. Bring up to simmering point, then cook over a gentle heat for about 10 minutes, stirring occasionally.

While the peperonata is cooking, cut polenta into 1/4-inch slices. Melt the butter or olive oil in another, preferably nonstick, skillet. Fry the polenta on each side until crisp and golden, 5–7 minutes.

Serves 4

mushrooms with potatoes

see variations page 218

Here's a rich, creamy, substantial supper dish that's wonderful to come home to on a winter's evening. To reduce the fat, make it with soy-based cream or reduced-fat cream — it's perfectly delicious. This is great on its own or served with grilled tomatoes or a tomato salad.

1 lb. new potatoes, halved or quartered if large
2 tbsp. olive oil
3 garlic cloves, peeled and halved
8 oz. mixed mushrooms, such as cremini, oyster, button, shiitake

3 sprigs fresh thyme (or 1 tsp. dried)
3/4 cup heavy cream
salt and black pepper

Bring a large saucepan of water to a boil, add the potatoes, and return to a boil. Cover and simmer for 15–20 minutes or until the potatoes are cooked. Drain.

Meanwhile, heat the olive oil in a small pan. Add the garlic, mushrooms, and thyme, and cook for 3–4 minutes, until the mushrooms have softened. Add the cream, season with salt and pepper to taste, then bring to a boil. Simmer until the liquid is reduced by about one-third, 7–10 minutes.

Slightly crush the potatoes and combine with the mushroom-cream mixture.

Serves 4

vegetarian chili

see variations page 219

This is a vegetarian staple, and for good reason: It's healthy, filling, and very economical to make — and, oh yes, very tasty, too! For a hotter chili, break open the chiles to release the seeds.

3 tbsp. sunflower oil
1 tsp. ground cumin
1 tsp. ground coriander
2 garlic cloves, minced
2 medium onions, sliced
1 red bell pepper, sliced
1 green bell pepper, sliced
1 large zucchini, cut into chunks

2 dried red chiles
1 (15-oz.) can chopped tomatoes
1/2 cup frozen or canned corn
2 tbsp. tomato paste
1 (15-oz.) can red kidney beans, washed and
    drained
1 tbsp. paprika
salt and black pepper

Heat the oil in a large saucepan and add the cumin, coriander, garlic, onions, bell peppers, zucchini, and chiles; cook for 3–4 minutes. Add the tomatoes, corn, tomato paste, and beans. Bring to a boil over a high heat, then reduce the heat and simmer for 15 minutes. Stir in the paprika and season with salt and pepper to taste. Serve with rice, crackers, or tortilla chips, and a side of sour cream.

Serves 4

pumpkin, garbanzo & prune tagine

see variations page 220

This quick and easy Moroccan-style stew is sophisticated enough to serve to discerning vegetarians and simple enough for a family meal. Serve with couscous.

3 tbsp. sunflower oil
1 medium red onion, finely chopped
1 garlic clove, minced
1 tsp. ground cumin
1 tsp. ground coriander
1/2 tsp. ground cinnamon
1 tbsp. harissa
10 oz. pumpkin or butternut squash, cut into
    3/4-inch chunks

10 oz. potato, cut into 3/4-inch chunks
1 (15-oz.) can tomatoes
1 cup vegetable bouillon
1 (15-oz.) can garbanzo beans
2/3 cup pitted prunes
2 medium zucchini, sliced
2 3/4 cups water
large pinch salt
1 1/2 cups couscous

Heat the oil in a tagine or large skillet. Cook the onion over medium heat for 3 minutes. Add the garlic and cook for 2 minutes. Add the cumin, coriander, cinnamon, and harissa, and cook for 1 minute. Add the pumpkin or butternut squash and the potato, and stir to coat in the spicy oil. Stir in the tomatoes, bouillon, and garbanzo beans. Cook for 10 minutes, stir in the prunes and zucchini, and cook for an additional 10 minutes.

Meanwhile, bring the water to a boil in a saucepan, add the salt and couscous, and remove from the heat. Cover with a clean kitchen cloth and let stand for 5 minutes. When all the water is absorbed, fluff with a fork and serve with the tagine.

Serves 4–5

huevos revueltos mexicali

see variations page 221

Scrambled eggs with tomatoes and chile make a great anytime meal. Serve on a corn tortilla, in a burrito, or in a taco shell, maybe with a side of refried beans and some chili sauce. If you are really pushed for time, replace the fresh vegetables in the recipe with 1 cup of warmed purchased salsa.

6 eggs
salt
1 tbsp. butter or lard
1 medium tomato, chopped

1/2 small white onion, chopped
1 garlic clove, minced
1–2 serrano chiles, deseeded and chopped
2 tbsp. chopped fresh cilantro

Break the eggs into a bowl and mix to break up; do not beat. Season with salt to taste.

Melt the butter or lard in a nonstick skillet. Add the tomato, onion, garlic, and chile. Cook, stirring frequently, until the excess juice from the tomatoes has been absorbed and the onions are soft, 4–5 minutes. Pour in the egg and cook, stirring constantly, until the eggs are set. Serve garnished with cilantro.

Serves 4

cauliflower & spinach curry

see variations page 222

A classic quick curry — the vegetables, coconut milk, and spices are well blended, but not fiery hot. Use the optional chile if you like your curry spicy. Serve with naan or flatbread, if you want a change from rice.

2 tbsp. oil
1 large onion, sliced
1 garlic clove
1/2-inch piece fresh ginger, peeled and minced
1 dried chile, optional
2 tbsp. medium curry powder, or to taste

1 medium head cauliflower, cut into small
    florets
1 (15-oz.) can chopped tomatoes
1 (15-oz.) can coconut milk
6 oz. baby spinach leaves
2 tbsp. lemon juice

Heat the oil in a saucepan. Add the onion and cook over medium heat for 3 minutes. Add the garlic and ginger, and cook for 2 minutes. Add the chile, if using, and curry powder, and cook for 1 minute. Stir in cauliflower and toss to coat in the spices. Stir in the tomatoes and coconut milk, and simmer for 12–15 minutes or until the cauliflower is tender but firm. Add the spinach and lemon juice, and cook for 2 minutes to wilt.

Serves 2

potato frittata

see variations page 223

This is a leftovers special: Cooked potatoes, a few fresh herbs, and some eggs are all you need to make a fine and filling meal. Use whatever vegetables are in the refrigerator to add to this wonderful egg dish. It can be served hot, warm, or at room temperature and is great for picnics.

1 tsp. olive oil
1 tsp. butter, melted
2 medium cooked potatoes, sliced
6 eggs

4 oz. crumbled feta or cheddar cheese
2 tbsp. chopped mixed fresh herbs (cilantro, basil, chives, dill, parsley)

Coat the bottom and sides of an ovenproof skillet with olive oil and melted butter. Put the potatoes into bottom of skillet and place on stove. Cook over medium heat until they begin to sizzle.

Preheat broiler.

In a bowl, whisk the eggs and stir in the cheese and herbs. Pour egg mixture on top of the potatoes, shaking to allow the egg to seep through the potatoes. Cook gently for 10 minutes; the frittata should be firm underneath, but still underdone on the top.

Transfer the skillet to the broiler and cook until set and browned on top, about 5 minutes.

Serves 4

mushroom & bamboo stir-fry

see variations page 224

With a hint of ginger and chili, this is a satisfying Chinese-influenced main course stir-fry. Serve with rice or noodles.

12 oz. mixed mushrooms (shiitake, oyster)
2 tsp. cornstarch
1 tbsp. water
3 tbsp. peanut or sunflower oil
1-inch piece fresh ginger, peeled and cut into fine matchsticks
1 garlic clove, finely chopped
2 tbsp. soy sauce

1/3 cup vegetable bouillon
1 tbsp. Chinese rice wine
1 tsp. honey
1/4 tsp. chili flakes
8 oz. canned bamboo shoots
2 green onions, finely sliced
1 tsp. sesame oil
sesame seeds, to garnish

Remove the stems from the mushrooms and wipe clean with damp paper towels. Mix the cornstarch to a paste with the water; set aside.

Put the wok on a high heat and add the oil. Stir fry ginger and garlic for 1 minute, add the mushrooms, and cook for 2-3 minutes until the mushrooms have given off their liquid. Add the soy sauce, bouillon, rice wine, honey, chili flakes, and cornstarch mixture. Bring to a boil, stirring until the sauce thickens. Add the bamboo shoots and heat through. Serve over rice sprinkled with green onions, sesame oil, and sesame seeds.

Serves 4

artichoke & zucchini tart

see variations page 225

Fresh or frozen pastry shells are fantastic if you're pressed for time. Make sure yours are sugar-free!

8 oz. cream cheese
1/2 cup sour cream
1/4 cup fresh chopped basil
1/2 cup sundried tomatoes, chopped, divided
1 (4-oz.) ball mozzarella, cut into small pieces, divided

salt and pepper
ready-made pastry shell
2 zucchini
8 oz. artichokes from a jar, drained and roughly chopped
flavored or regular olive oil

Preheat the oven to 375°F.

In a bowl, mix the cream cheese, sour cream, basil, half the sundried tomatoes, half the mozzarella, and salt and pepper to taste. Spread into the pastry shell. Using a peeler, cut the zucchini into fine ribbons and lay on top of the cheese mixture with the artichokes, remaining sundried tomatoes, and remaining mozzarella. Drizzle with olive oil.

Bake for 15 minutes until the vegetables are crisp at the edges and the pastry shell is golden.

Serves 4

piquant bean stew

see variations page 226

Canned beans and a jar of piquillo peppers combine to give spark to this quick supper dish. Serve on a bed of rice pilaf or couscous for a sensational supper.

2 tbsp. olive oil
1 medium red onion, sliced
3 garlic cloves, minced
1/2 (8-oz.) jar roasted piquillo peppers, drained
1 (15-oz.) can cannellini beans
1 (15-oz.) can black beans
1/2 tsp. red chili flakes

1 tbsp. chopped fresh oregano or marjoram
1/2 cup vegetable bouillon
1 tbsp. tomato paste
4 oz. baby spinach
2 tsp. lime juice
salt and black pepper

Heat the oil in a saucepan. Add the onion and cook over medium heat for 3 minutes. Add the garlic and cook for 2 minutes, until soft. Add the piquilo peppers, beans, chili, oregano or marjoram, bouillon, and tomato paste; cook for 5 minutes. Stir in the spinach and cook for 2 minutes, until wilted. Stir in the lime juice and add salt and black pepper to taste.

Serves 4

goat cheese, tomato & avocado omelet

see variations page 227

This is the best omelet filling ever! Scale up the recipe if making for more than yourself, but serve as soon as the omelets are cooked or they will lose some of their fluffiness. For the perfect feel-good supper, serve with some leftover potatoes, fried to a crisp with a little finely sliced onion, and an arugula salad.

2 eggs
1 tbsp. water
salt and pepper
1 tbsp. butter

5 grape tomatoes, halved lengthwise
1/4 avocado, peeled, pitted, and sliced
2 tbsp. goat cheese, crumbled

Preheat the broiler.

Beat the eggs in a mixing bowl with the water and salt and pepper to taste. Warm the serving plate.

Heat the butter in a medium nonstick skillet; when foaming, pour in the egg mixture. Stir, gently drawing the mixture from the set edge toward the center as it sets. When almost set, add the tomatoes, avocado, and goat cheese; cook for 1 minute. Put under the hot broiler and cook the top of the omelet until it is just set, about 2 minutes. Fold in half.

Serves 1

peperonata with crispy polenta

see base recipe page 199

peperonata-stuffed crepes
Prepare the basic recipe, omitting the polenta. Take 8 ready-made crepes and divide the peperonata among them, placing the filling down the center. Roll up and put in a baking pan. Sprinkle 2 ounces shredded cheddar cheese on top and bake in a 350°F oven until the cheese turns golden, about 10 minutes.

peperonata with linguine
Prepare the basic recipe, omitting the polenta. Cook 12 ounces linguine following the package instructions. Serve the peperonata over the linguine, sprinkled with Parmesan cheese.

peperonata with fried egg
Prepare the basic recipe. In a skillet, melt 1 tablespoon butter. Crack in four eggs and fry to your liking. Serve on top of the peperonata. Buttered toast may be substituted for polenta, if desired.

peperonata with white beans
Prepare the basic recipe. Five minutes before the end of the cooking time add 1 (15-ounce) can drained and rinsed cannellini beans.

variations

mushrooms with potatoes

see base recipe page 201

potato, bean & chestnut casserole
Prepare the basic recipe, using only 4 ounces quartered cremini mushrooms
and cooking a sliced red onion with the garlic and mushrooms. Add 1 cup
halved canned chestnuts and 1 cup pinto beans with the cream.

potato, cheese & onion casserole
Prepare the basic recipe, replacing the mushrooms with 2 medium sliced
white onions. When the sauce is reduced, stir in 3 ounces shredded fontina,
Monterey Jack, or cheddar cheese, and heat gently until just melted.

potato, mushroom & tomato casserole
Prepare the basic recipe, replacing cream with 1 (15-ounce) can tomato
sauce. Simmer for just 5 minutes.

potato & corn casserole
Prepare the basic recipe, omitting mushrooms and softening 1 sliced red
onion in the olive oil. Add 1 cup canned or frozen corn and 1/4 of a red bell
pepper, cut into small chunks.

variations

vegetarian chili

see base recipe page 202

vegetarian taco salad
Prepare the basic recipe; cool until warm. Meanwhile, in a large bowl, put 14 ounces tortilla chips, 1 1/2 cups shredded lettuce, 3 ounces shredded Monterey Jack cheese, 2 large chopped tomatoes, 1/4 cup fresh chopped cilantro, and 1/2 cup salsa. Mix with the bean mixture and top with sour cream, accompanied by lime wedges.

spiced bean, vegetable & lentil stew
Prepare the basic recipe, adding 1 cup canned lentils with the tomatoes.

spiced peanutty black bean stew
Prepare the basic recipe, omitting the zucchini and paprika, and using only 1 tablespoon of tomato paste. Replace kidney beans with drained and rinsed black beans, and stir 2 tablespoons peanut butter into the finished stew.

curried bean stew with ginger
Prepare the basic recipe, omitting corn and tomato paste. Replace cumin and coriander with 2–3 teaspoons medium curry powder, and add 2 teaspoons minced fresh ginger with the garlic.

variations

pumpkin, garbanzo & prune tagine

see base recipe page 205

sweet potato, pumpkin & prune tagine
Prepare the basic recipe, replacing the potato with sweet potato.

pumpkin, garbanzo & prune tagine with bitter lemon & olives
Prepare the basic recipe, adding 1 preserved lemon, quartered and seeds removed, and 3/4 cup pitted green olives with the tomatoes.

pumpkin, garbanzo & apricot tagine
Prepare the basic recipe, replacing the prunes with dried apricots.

pumpkin, green bean, garbanzo & prune tagine
Prepare the basic recipe, replacing the potatoes with 8 ounces trimmed and halved green beans. Bitter lemon and olives may be added, if desired, as directed above.

variations

huevos revueltos mexicali

see base recipe page 206

huevos revueltos española
Prepare the basic recipe, omitting the vegetables. Add 6 ounces each of baby spinach and cooked shrimp. Cook until the shrimp is heated and the spinach is limp; drain excess liquid. Add the eggs and proceed as directed.

huevos revueltos peperonata
Prepare the basic recipe, replacing the vegetables with 1 cup prepared peperonata (page 199). Add the eggs and proceed as directed.

chorizo huevos revueltos
Prepare the basic recipe, omitting the tomatoes and chile. Remove the sausage casings, then crumble 6 ounces of chorizo and cook with the onion in the skillet until browned. Add the eggs and proceed as directed.

ricotta huevos revueltos
Prepare the basic recipe, adding 1 tablespoon chopped chives with the salt. When cooked, add 1/2 cup ricotta cheese to the scrambled egg and stir gently while heating through, leaving small lumps of cheese intact.

variations

cauliflower & spinach curry

see base recipe page 207

sweet potato & spinach curry
Prepare the basic recipe, replacing the cauliflower with 3 sweet potatoes, peeled and cut into 1-inch chunks.

green bean & spinach curry
Prepare the basic recipe, replacing the cauliflower with 1 pound trimmed green beans.

okra curry
Prepare the basic recipe, omitting the cauliflower, spinach, and coconut milk. Add 12 ounces okra, washed, trimmed and cut into 3/4-inch pieces, and 1 small chopped green bell pepper with the tomatoes. Cook for about 10 minutes until the okra is tender but not mushy.

mixed vegetable curry
Prepare the basic recipe, omitting the cauliflower and using frozen spinach. Add 12 ounces frozen mixed vegetables with the tomatoes and cook for 10 minutes. Add 6 ounces frozen spinach, thawed and squeezed dry, and heat through.

variations

potato frittata

see base recipe page 208

zucchini frittata
Prepare the basic recipe, omitting the potatoes. Cook 1 small sliced onion and
1 large sliced zucchini in the skillet until soft. Proceed as directed.

potato & bacon frittata
Prepare the basic recipe, but cook 4 strips of bacon, cut into 1/4-inch pieces, in
the oil (omit butter) in the pan before adding the potatoes to the bacon
drippings. Proceed as directed.

spinach & blue cheese frittata
Prepare the basic recipe, omitting the potatoes and wilting 4 ounces baby
spinach in the skillet. Add 10 halved grape tomatoes. Replace the feta or
cheddar with 4 ounces crumbled blue cheese.

potato & smoked salmon frittata
Prepare the basic recipe, adding 2 ounces smoked salmon bits to the potatoes
before adding the egg. Use feta cheese and dill or chives.

variations

mushroom & bamboo stir-fry

see base recipe page 211

mushroom & broccoli stir-fry

Prepare the basic recipe, omitting the bamboo shoots. Cut the florets from a medium-size head of broccoli and blanch for 2 minutes. Drain and toss into the stir-fry as the mushroom liquid is reducing.

mushroom & cashew stir-fry

Prepare the basic recipe. Add 3/4 cup toasted, unsalted cashew nuts once the mushroom liquid has been reduced.

mushroom & bean sprout stir-fry

Prepare the basic recipe, replacing bamboo shoots with 8 ounces bean sprouts.

dried mushroom stir-fry

Prepare the basic recipe, replacing the mushrooms with 10 Chinese (black) mushrooms. Rehydrate the dried mushrooms by soaking in hot water for 20 minutes. Squeeze out excess water and slice. Pour the soaking water through a sieve lined with a paper towel; use in place of the bouillon.

variations

artichoke & zucchini tart

see base recipe page 212

peperonata tart
Prepare the basic recipe, omitting the artichoke and zucchini. Top the tart with red and yellow charbroiled peppers from a jar, drained and sliced, and the remaining tomatoes and remaining mozzarella. Proceed as directed.

asparagus tart
Prepare the basic recipe, omitting the remaining half of the sundried tomatoes, the artichoke, and the zucchini. Blanch 12 ounces asparagus in boiling water for 2 minutes; drain and refresh in cold water, then dry. Arrange in the pastry shell. Top with Parmesan cheese. Proceed as directed.

tomato tart
Prepare the basic recipe, omitting the remaining half of the sundried tomatoes, the artichoke, and the zucchini. Top the tart with 8 ounces baby roma tomatoes, or grape tomatoes, halved lengthwise. Proceed as directed.

green onion & potato tart
Prepare the basic recipe, omitting the remaining half of the sundried tomatoes, the artichoke, and the zucchini. Top the tart with 3 sliced cooked potatoes and 4 fat green onions, trimmed, sliced lengthwise, and laid cut-side up. Brush with olive oil. Proceed as directed.

variations

piquant bean stew

see base recipe page 215

bean & tomato stew
Prepare the basic recipe, omitting the piquillo peppers and adding 1 cup
chopped canned tomatoes and 1/4 cup each chopped sundried tomatoes
and pitted green olives with the beans.

piquant garbanzo stew
Prepare the basic recipe, replacing the cannellini beans and black beans with
2 (15-ounce) cans garbanzo beans.

grilled chicken with piquant beans
Prepare the basic recipe. Use as the base for a piece of grilled chicken with
lemon and thyme, page 105.

piquant bean, corn & potato stew
Prepare the basic recipe, omitting the cannellini beans and adding 1 cup
corn and 1 medium or large cooked and chopped potato.

variations

goat cheese, tomato & avocado omelet

see base recipe page 216

blue cheese, tomato & avocado omelet
Prepare the basic recipe, replacing the goat cheese with Gorgonzola or
Roquefort cheese.

mexican omelet
Prepare the basic recipe, replacing the goat cheese and tomatoes with
Monterey Jack and 1/4 cup salsa.

goat cheese, tomato, avocado & spinach omelet
Prepare the basic recipe, adding 1 cup torn baby spinach leaves to the
egg mixture.

bacon, tomato & avocado omelet
Prepare the basic recipe, omitting the goat cheese. In a nonstick skillet, cook
2 slices of bacon (or vegetarian "bacon," if desired) until crisp over medium
heat; drain on paper towels, then crumble and set aside. Proceed as directed,
adding the crumbled bacon with the tomato and avocado.

side dishes

The value of a good side dish should never be underestimated. Rice and grain dishes, common and seasonal vegetables can all add panache to your plate. Think color, think texture, think surprise when choosing a side dish to complement your entrée.

Our selection contains familiar dishes, but updated and uplifted with a few carefully chosen ingredients to give your cooking an edge.

rice pilaf

see variations page 244

It takes little effort and only a few extra minutes to transform plain old rice into something vibrant and tasty. If you happen to have homemade broth, that's a bonus, but a bouillon cube is what's on hand for most of us! This rice is delicious with meat, fish, or vegetable main dishes and can also be served cold as a salad.

1 tbsp. olive oil
1 tbsp. butter
2 shallots or 1 small onion, finely chopped
1 celery stick, sliced in half lengthwise and
    finely chopped
1 1/3 cups long grain or basmati rice

2 2/3 cups boiling water
1 chicken or vegetable bouillon cube
salt and black pepper
1 tsp. grated lemon zest
2 tbsp. fresh chopped herbs such as parsley or
    cilantro

In a saucepan, heat the oil and butter over medium heat. Add the shallots or onion and celery, and cook until soft, stirring frequently. Add the rice and turn to coat in the fat; cook until translucent, turning constantly. Pour in the boiling water and crumble in the bouillon cube. Season with salt and pepper to taste, keeping in mind that bouillon cubes are quite salty. Return to a boil, reduce the heat, cover, and simmer for about 12 minutes, or according to the package directions. If the rice becomes dry before it is cooked, add an additional 1/4 cup water.

Remove the saucepan from the heat and let the rice steam, covered, for 5 minutes or until rice is cooked through. Fluff with a fork and stir in the lemon zest and herbs.

Serves 4

harissa couscous

see variations page 245

Nothing could be simpler or easier than cooking couscous. Harissa is the bright red, fiery chili paste that is used in North African cooking and it gives this recipe some heat. Omit if that is not to your taste. Serve hot with a tagine or stew, or cold as a salad — in which case, add the green onions, tomatoes, and herbs once the couscous has cooled.

2 cups couscous
1 vegetable or chicken bouillon cube
2 cups boiling water
1 tsp. harissa paste
4 green onions, sliced

1 large deseeded chopped tomato
1/4 cup chopped fresh mint (or half mint and half parsley)
3 tbsp. olive oil
juice of 1 lemon

Put the couscous in a heatproof bowl. Dissolve the bouillon cube in the boiling water and stir in the harissa. Pour over the couscous and stir well. Cover the bowl with a damp dishtowel and leave for 5 minutes. The couscous should be soft. Fluff with a fork. Stir in the green onions, tomato, mint, olive oil, and lemon juice.

Serves 4

warm quinoa with bacon & peas

see variations page 246

Quinoa is not just for salads; it makes a good accompaniment, too. This hot quinoa is great with a simple meat dish, such as lamb or pork chops.

1 cup quinoa, rinsed
2 cups water or vegetable bouillon
salt and black pepper
1/2 cup frozen peas
3 strips of smoked bacon, chopped

1 small onion, chopped
1/2 red bell pepper, chopped
1/2–1 jalapeño chile, sliced
1 large tomato, skinned, deseeded, and chopped

Put the quinoa and water or bouillon in a saucepan over high heat. Add a generous pinch of salt and black pepper to taste, stir, then bring to a boil. Reduce the boil and simmer over low heat for 10 minutes. Add the peas, return to a simmer, then cook, stirring occasionally, until all of the water has been absorbed, 5–10 minutes. Remove the quinoa from the heat. Fluff with a fork.

Meanwhile, cook the bacon in a skillet over medium heat until it releases its fat. Add the onion, bell pepper, and jalapeño chile, and cook until the onion is soft. Stir in the tomato and heat through; do not allow to become mushy.

Stir the bacon and vegetable mixture into the quinoa, and adjust the seasoning to taste.

Serves 4

lemon & mustard cabbage

see variations page 247

Ready in less than 5 minutes, this is a great vegetable side dish. Although it is Indian-inspired, it works well with simple meat and fish dishes from most cuisines.

1 tbsp. sunflower oil
1 tbsp. mustard seeds
1/2 head green cabbage, cored and sliced
juice of 1/2 lemon
salt and black pepper

In a large skillet or wok, heat the oil over medium-high heat. Add the mustard seeds, and when they start to pop, immediately add the cabbage. Stir-fry until the cabbage is tender-crisp, 3–4 minutes. Pour in the lemon juice and season with salt and pepper to taste.

Serves 4

garlic mash

see variations page 248

The ultimate comfort food: creamy mashed potatoes with garlic. You can stir in 1/4 cup shredded Parmesan cheese for a richer version, too. Fry it up for breakfast with bacon and egg, or serve with a steak.

1 lb. potatoes, peeled
2–3 garlic cloves, peeled
1/4 cup half and half
2 tbsp. olive oil or butter
salt and black pepper

Cut the potatoes into even-size pieces, put in a saucepan with the garlic, and cover with water. Bring to a boil, cover, and simmer for about 20 minutes, until the potatoes are tender. Mash with a potato masher or press through a ricer; do not use a food processor or you will end up with a gluey texture. Warm the half and half with the oil or butter in a small pan or in the microwave, and stir into the potatoes, adding salt and pepper to taste.

Serves 4

balsamic zucchini ribbons

see variations page 249

How easy is this? A lovely accompaniment to a simple fish or meat dish. Let it cool and you've got a wonderful salad dish, too.

4 medium zucchini
1/4 cup flavored olive oil, divided
salt and black pepper
2 tbsp. balsamic vinegar
2 tbsp. fresh chopped basil

Preheat the broiler. Line the broiler pan with aluminum foil and drizzle with olive oil.

Using a mandolin slicer or a sharp knife, slice the zucchini lengthwise into 1/4-inch-thick slices. Put the zucchini in the broiler pan and brush with more oil. Season generously with salt and pepper to taste. Place the pan 4 inches away from the heat source and broil for 5–6 minutes, until tender and golden brown. Drizzle with vinegar and serve sprinkled with basil.

Serves 4

hot beet & sour cream salad

see variations page 250

The beet is an overlooked vegetable, but so tasty with meat or fish. What's more, the supermarkets have done the work for us, so we can purchase beets peeled and cooked — ready to use.

8 oz. cooked beets, diced
1 tsp. Djion mustard
1 tsp. honey
1/4 cup apple cider vinegar

1 cup sour cream
salt and black pepper
2 tbsp. chopped fresh dill

Put the diced beets into a small saucepan. In a bowl, combine the mustard, honey, and apple cider vinegar. Pour over the beets, bring to a boil, and cook for 2 minutes. Stir in the sour cream and heat through. Add salt and pepper to taste. Serve sprinkled with chopped dill.

Serves 4

sautéed chard with swiss cheese

see variations page 251

The French way of serving this homey vegetable makes it into something quite special, although simple enough for an everyday meal. The stalks are separated from the leaves and cooked for a few minutes longer to ensure that both parts of the plant are cooked to perfection.

1 (1-lb.) bunch Swiss chard
1 tbsp. butter
1 tbsp. olive oil
1 shallot or half a small onion, chopped
1 garlic clove, minced
1/2 cup white wine or vegetable bouillon

2 tbsp. half and half or yogurt
1 tsp. paprika
1/3 cup shredded Swiss cheese or Emmental cheese, divided
salt and black pepper

To prepare the chard, cut out the central ribs with the stems; roughly chop the stalks into 1/4-inch. slices, and roughly chop the leaves.

In a large skillet, melt the butter and olive oil. Add the shallot or onion and cook for 3 minutes, then add the garlic and cook for 2 minutes. Stir in the chard stalks and wine or bouillon, and cook, stirring occasionally, until the stems begin to soften. Add the leaves and cook until they wilt and are just tender-crisp. Stir in the half and half or yogurt, paprika, and 1/4 cup of cheese. Heat through, add salt and pepper to taste, and serve sprinkled with the remaining cheese.

Serves 4

corn fritters

see variations page 252

This is a light version of the corn fritter that uses very little flour. It goes well with grilled chicken, bacon-wrapped steak, or sausages. It's a good side dish to offer a mixed meat and vegetarian crowd, as vegetarians can make a meal of it.

1 egg
2 tbsp. all-purpose flour
2 cups frozen corn, thawed and drained, or
    cooked kernels from 2 large ears of corn

1/2 tsp. chili flakes, optional
salt and white pepper
1 egg white
1 tbsp. butter

In a bowl, beat the egg and flour. Stir in the corn and chili flakes, if using, and add salt and pepper to taste. In a separate bowl, beat the egg white until it becomes stiff, then carefully turn into the corn mixture using a spatula.

Heat the butter in a large skillet and add tablespoons of the mixture. Cook for 2–3 minutes on each side until golden. Repeat until the mixture is used up. Drain on paper towels before serving at once.

Makes 7–8 fritters

greek-style green beans

see variations page 253

Plain green beans are given a lift with the addition of tomatoes, onions, and herbs. Do not be afraid of the olive oil; it's authentically Greek and makes the beans tender and delicious. Leftovers are good as a cold salad.

1 lb. fresh green beans, trimmed
1/3 cup olive oil
1 medium onion, sliced
1 garlic clove, minced
1 teaspoon dried oregano

3 roma tomatoes, peeled and diced, or 1 (8-oz.)
    can chopped tomatoes
1/2 tsp. sugar
2 tbsp. chopped fresh parsley

Cook the green beans in a saucepan of boiling water for 3 minutes; drain.

Meanwhile, heat the olive oil in a saucepan and cook the onion for 3 minutes. Add the garlic and oregano, and continue to cook until the onion is soft. Add the tomatoes and sugar, and heat through. Stir the cooked beans into the tomato mixture and cook for 10 minutes. Serve sprinkled with fresh parsley.

Serves 4

variations

rice pilaf

see base recipe page 229

toasted almond rice
Prepare the basic recipe, adding 1/4 cup toasted slivered almonds to the
finished rice with the parsley. Good with Middle Eastern and Asian dishes,
particularly fish and lamb.

sesame rice pilaf
Prepare the basic recipe, replacing half the olive oil with sesame oil. Once
the onions have softened, stir in 1 teaspoon minced fresh, peeled gingerroot
and cook for 1 minute. Replace the fresh herbs and lemon zest with
1 tablespoon lightly toasted sesame seeds and 1 finely chopped green onion.
Good with Chinese and Thai dishes.

raisin–lemon millet pilaf
Prepare the basic recipe, replacing the rice with 1 cup washed millet and
using 2 cups boiling water. Proceed as directed. The millet should have
absorbed all the water after simmering about 15–20 minutes. If it becomes
dry before it is cooked, add an additional 1/4 cup water. Stir in 1/4 cup
raisins and 1 tablespoon lemon juice with the herbs.

variations

harissa couscous

see base recipe page 231

couscous with mixed seeds
Prepare couscous in the bouillon (harissa optional) as directed, omitting tomatoes. While couscous rests, dry-toast 1/4 cup each of sunflower and pumpkin seeds, and 2 tablespoons sesame seeds. Stir into couscous.

couscous with dukka
Prepare dukka by dry-toasting 1/4 cup each of sesame seeds and almonds. Add 2 tablespoons coriander seeds and 1 teaspoon cumin seeds; toast for 1 minute. Cool, then grind to a powder in a food processor. Prepare the couscous as directed, omitting tomatoes and harissa. Sprinkle finished dish with dukka. Serve warm or cold.

harissa bulgar wheat
Prepare the basic recipe, replacing the couscous with medium grain washed bulgar wheat. The bulgar will take 10–15 minutes to absorb the water. Drain off excess water; fluff with a fork. Proceed as directed. Serve warm or cold.

spicy harissa buckwheat
Prepare the basic recipe, replacing the couscous with roasted buckwheat. Put the buckwheat in a saucepan and add the boiling bouillon mixture; simmer for 15–20 minutes until tender. Proceed as directed. Serve warm or cold.

warm quinoa with bacon & peas

see base recipe page 232

quinoa with hot balsamic dressing
Prepare the basic recipe, omitting the bacon and adding 1 tablespoon of olive oil to the skillet before adding the onions. Combine 1/4 cup each of olive oil and balsamic vinegar with 1 tablespoon Dijon mustard and 1/2 teaspoon of garlic powder. Pour over the finished dish and cook for a couple of minutes to heat through.

quinoa with mushrooms
Prepare the basic recipe, omitting the bacon and adding 1 tablespoon of olive oil to the skillet before the onions. With the other vegetables add 4 ounces small button mushrooms.

quinoa with mixed vegetables
Prepare the quinoa as directed, omitting the other ingredients. Cook 2 cups frozen vegetable medley as directed on the package, and add to the hot quinoa with the juice of 1/2 lemon and 2 tablespoons fresh chopped basil.

quinoa with black beans
Prepare the basic recipe, omitting bacon and adding 1 tablespoon of olive oil to the skillet before the onions. Add 1 (15-ounce) can drained and washed black beans to the quinoa 5 minutes before it is cooked. Proceed as directed.

lemon & mustard cabbage

see base recipe page 234

cabbage with lemon & dill
Prepare the basic recipe, omitting the mustard seeds. With the cabbage add
2 teaspoons dried dill and proceed as directed. If using chopped fresh dill,
use 2 tablespoons and add with the lemon.

cabbage with bacon & caraway seeds
Prepare the basic recipe, omitting mustard seeds and lemon. To the hot oil add
2 strips smoked bacon, chopped, and cook until it has released its fat, then add
1 small sliced onion and stir-fry 2 minutes. Add 1 minced garlic clove and
1 tablespoon caraway seeds; stir-fry 1 minute. Add cabbage; proceed as directed.

cabbage with orange & poppy seeds
Prepare the basic recipe, omitting mustard seeds and lemon. Once the cabbage
is cooked, add the zest and juice of 1/2 orange mixed with 1 teaspoon Dijon
mustard, 1 tablespoon poppy seeds, and 1 teaspoon balsamic vinegar. Toss and
add salt and pepper to taste.

cabbage with garlic & soy
Prepare the basic recipe, omitting mustard seeds and lemon. To the hot oil add
2 minced garlic cloves and cook for 1 minute. Proceed as directed, replacing
the lemon with 2 tablespoons light soy sauce.

variations

garlic mash

see base recipe page 235

celeriac mash
Prepare the basic recipe, omitting the garlic, if desired. In a separate saucepan, put 1 pound celeriac, peeled and cut into 1-inch pieces. Cover with water and add 1 tablespoon lemon juice. Bring to a boil, then simmer for about 15 minutes, until tender. Drain; purée in a blender until smooth. Add the celeriac to the mashed potatoes and proceed as directed.

grainy mustard mash
Prepare the basic recipe, omitting the garlic. Stir 2–3 tablespoons grainy mustard into the finished mashed potatoes.

goat cheese mash
Prepare the basic recipe, omitting the garlic. With the cream add 4 ounces soft goat cheese and mash until well blended. Stir 2 tablespoons chopped fresh chives into the finished mashed potatoes.

pesto mash
Prepare the basic recipe, omitting the garlic. Stir 1–2 tablespoons basil pesto into the finished mashed potatoes.

variations

balsamic zucchini ribbons

see base recipe page 236

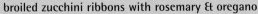

broiled zucchini ribbons with rosemary & oregano
Prepare the basic recipe, sprinkling the zucchini with 1 tablespoon chopped
fresh rosemary (1 teaspoon dried) and 1 teaspoon fresh chopped oregano
(1 generous pinch dried) before cooking.

broiled parmesan zucchini
Prepare the basic recipe, sprinkling the zucchini with 1/2 cup shredded
Parmesan cheese before cooking.

broiled lemon zucchini
Prepare the basic recipe, but sprinkle with the grated zest of 1/2 lemon before
cooking and replace the balsamic vinegar with lemon juice.

zucchini wraps
Prepare the basic recipe, but cook only 8 slices zucchini. Simultaneously broil
4 roma tomatoes, cut in half lengthwise. Cut 1 (4-ounce) ball mozzarella
cheese into 8 slices. When the zucchini is cooked, wrap 1/2 tomato, 1 cheese
slice, and 1 whole basil leaf in a cooked zucchini slice; repeat.

variations

hot beet & sour cream salad

see base recipe page 239

spiced hot beets
Prepare the basic recipe, omitting sour cream. Increase honey to
1 tablespoon, and with the apple cider vinegar add 1 teaspoon each
cardamom and chili flakes, and 1/2 teaspoon each garlic powder and
caraway seeds. Proceed as directed.

cold beet salad with sour cream
Prepare the beets as directed and put in a serving bowl. Cook the apple cider
vinegar, mustard, and sugar as directed and pour over beets; cool. Stir in the
sour cream and sprinkle with dill.

hot garlic beets with sour cream
In a small pan, cook 1 small chopped red onion for 3 minutes. Add 2 minced
garlic cloves and cook for 2 minutes, until soft. Add the beets and proceed
as directed, replacing Dijon mustard with 1 tablespoon grainy mustard.

hot horseradish beets with sour cream
Prepare basic recipe; add 2–3 tablespoons horseradish sauce with the vinegar.

sautéed chard with swiss cheese

see base recipe page 240

sautéed chard with orange
Prepare the basic recipe, omitting the half and half and cheese.
Add 1 teaspoon grated orange zest and 1 teaspoon orange juice in place of the
wine or bouillon.

creamy chard pasta
Prepare the basic recipe, increasing the half and half to 1 cup. When adding
the half and half, boil for 2 minutes, then proceed as directed, increasing the
cheese to 1 cup. Toss with cooked penne.

chard au gratin
Prepare the basic recipe; preheat the broiler. Instead of sprinkling 2 tablespoons
cheese on top, increase to 1/4 cup and mix with 1/2 cup soft breadcrumbs; add
salt and pepper to taste. Put the cooked chard in cream in a shallow heatproof
dish, sprinkle the bread mixture on top, and cook under the broiler until the
topping turns golden brown.

sautéed kale with swiss cheese
Prepare the basic recipe, replacing the chard with 1 1/2 pounds kale. Roughly
chop the stems and leaves of the kale, then proceed as directed.

variations

corn fritters

see base recipe page 242

corn, onion, chili & tomato fritters
Prepare the basic recipe, adding 1 thinly sliced green onion and 3 finely chopped sundried tomatoes with the corn.

corn & cheese fritters
Prepare the basic recipe, adding 1/2 cup shredded cheddar or Monterey Jack cheese with the corn.

zucchini fritters
Prepare the basic recipe, replacing corn with 2 cups shredded zucchini that has been squeezed dry using paper towels.

cheese & herb fritters
Prepare the basic recipe, replacing the corn with 1/2 cup shredded cheddar or Monterey Jack cheese and 1/2 cup chopped fresh mixed herbs such as parsley, basil, chive, cilantro, mint, and sage.

greek-style green beans

see base recipe page 243

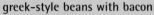

greek-style beans with bacon
Prepare the basic recipe. Add 3 chopped strips of smoked bacon to the
hot skillet; once the fat has started to run, add the olive oil and onion.
Proceed as directed.

greek-style lima beans
Prepare the basic recipe, replacing the green beans with 1 pound frozen lima
beans, cooked until tender.

green bean & tomato pasta
Prepare the basic recipe, doubling the tomatoes. Toss with cooked fusilli, then
sprinkle with Parmesan cheese.

greek-style potatoes
Prepare the basic recipe, replacing the green beans with 1 pound potatoes,
boiled, chopped into chunks, and cooked until just tender.

desserts

Sweet and creamy or fresh and fruity, a great
dessert doesn't need to be a labor of love to be a
crowd-pleaser. This chapter includes hot, cold, and
frozen desserts; a few are decadent treats, and
several are downright good for you! There are
desserts to impress and others that are simple, tasty
family fare — in fact, something for every occasion.

crispy apricot toasts

see variations page 272

This dessert is so easy to prepare and, as it can be made with canned fruit, is a great standby. Serve with yogurt, vanilla ice cream, or whipped cream, if desired.

4 large slices of white bread
4 tsp. butter
1 tsp. cinnamon

1/4 cup plus 4 tsp. demerara or brown sugar
8 ripe apricots or 1 (15-oz.) can apricot halves

Preheat oven to 350°F.

Remove the crusts from the bread. Spread thickly with butter, then sprinkle with cinnamon and 1/4 cup demerara or brown sugar. Put on a baking sheet.

Cut the apricots in half and remove the pits. Put 4 apricot halves on each slice of bread cut side up and sprinkle the remaining sugar on top. Bake for 15–20 minutes, until the bread is crisp and the fruit softened. Cut each slice into quarters and serve hot.

Serves 4

spiced apple & cranberry tartlets

see variations page 273

Using phyllo pastry means you can whip up apple tarts in no time. For an even quicker variation, replace the apples with applesauce.

2 sheets phyllo pastry
2 tsp. melted butter
1/3 cup brown sugar
1 tbsp. lemon juice
1/2 tsp. cinnamon

3 medium apples, sliced
1/3 cup cranberries
2 tbsp. chopped, toasted pecans
1 1/2 tbsp. confectioners' sugar

Preheat oven to 400°F.

Very lightly oil a 6-cup muffin pan. Lay 1 sheet of phyllo pastry on a cutting board and brush with melted butter. Using a sharp knife or scissors, cut width-wise into 3 5-inch slices. Fold each slice 3 times to make a square, then cut off the corners. Carefully mold each square into a muffin cup. Repeat with second sheet of phyllo. Bake for 5 minutes till golden.

Meanwhile, put the brown sugar, lemon juice, and cinnamon in a skillet, and cook until just simmering. Add the apple slices and cranberries, and cook, stirring often, until the apples are tender, about 5 minutes. Spoon the apple mixture into the phyllo shells. Top with the pecans and then the confectioners' sugar.

Serves 6

chocolate cake mousse with cherries

see variations page 274

Everyone loves chocolate mousse and chocolate muffins; in this dessert, they are decadently combined. This dish contains uncooked eggs, so it should not be given to pregnant women or to the immune-suppressed.

2 chocolate muffins, cut into chunks
1/4 cup chocolate milk or Bailey's liqueur
2 oz. semisweet chocolate
2 eggs, separated
pinch salt

1/2 cup sugar
2/3 cup heavy cream
few drops almond extract
chocolate shavings, to serve

Divide the chunks of chocolate muffin into the base of 4 serving bowls. Moisten with the chocolate milk or Bailey's liqueur.

Melt the chocolate in a bowl over a saucepan of simmering water; cool slightly. Meanwhile, in 3 separate bowls using clean beaters, whisk the egg whites and salt until stiff, but not dry, then beat the egg yolks, and sugar until light and fluffy; and whisk the cream until thick.

Carefully blend 1/3 of the melted chocolate into the egg yolk mixture, then gently fold in the remaining chocolate, followed by the almond extract, the whipped cream, and finally the egg whites, taking care not to overwork the mixture. Pile on top of the muffin chunks. Serve garnished with chocolate shavings.

Serves 4

cherry hot fudge sundaes

see variations page 275

Use good-quality cherries for this recipe — those in a jar are best, and for special occasions, use cherries in liquor and serve accompanied by amoretti, tuiles, or mini meringues. For an even quicker sauce, see the coconut–chocolate variation, page 275.

for the sauce
1 cup semisweet chocolate chips
2 tbsp. butter
1 (14-oz.) can sweetened evaporated milk
1 tsp. vanilla extract
2 tbsp. water

8 small scoops vanilla ice cream
1 (14-oz.) jar or can pitted cherries
whipped cream, to garnish

In a saucepan, combine all the sauce ingredients. Slowly bring to a simmer; cook 3 minutes.

Layer scoops of ice cream, cherries (reserving 4 for the topping), and chocolate sauce in heatproof glasses. Top with the whipped cream and the reserved cherries.

Serves 4

jeweled persian yogurt parfaits

see variations page 276

This elegant, healthy dessert is very beautiful to look at, with a sensational taste that matches. Pomegranate seeds can be frozen and kept for several months in the freezer; they can be used from frozen in this dessert.

1 pint Greek-style yogurt
1 tbsp. rosewater or orange flower water
1/4–1/2 cup liquid honey, divided

1 cup pomegranate seeds
1/2 cup pistachios, chopped
fresh rose petals or mint leaves, to garnish

In a bowl, combine the yogurt and rosewater or orange flower water, then add the honey to taste, reserving 4 teaspoons for the topping. Fill 4 dessert glasses, alternating layers of yogurt, pomegranate seeds, and pistachios. Drizzle 1 teaspoon of honey over the top of each dessert, and serve garnished with fresh rose petals or mint leaves.

Serves 4

mock berry brûlée

see variations page 277

Okay, not quite the real thing, but still a decadent and impressive dessert! Serve with shortcake cookies.

1 1/3 cups fresh mixed berries, or semi-thawed, if frozen
4 tsp. superfine sugar, or to taste
1 package (3 oz.) vanilla instant pudding

1/2 cup chilled whipping cream
2 tbsp. Kahlua, optional
1/2 cup brown sugar
rolled cookies, to serve

Preheat broiler before serving.

Divide the berries among 4 heatproof ramekin dishes, sprinkle with sugar, then set aside.

Prepare the vanilla pudding as directed. Beat the cream until stiff, but not dry, then fold into the pudding mix. Stir in Kahlua, if using. Spoon the mixture on top of the berries in the ramekin dishes. The dish can be made to this point and refrigerated until needed.

Just before serving, sprinkle the brown sugar over the ramekins and broil about 5 inches away from the heat, until the sugar melts and begins to caramelize. Alternatively, caramelize the sugar using a cook's blowtorch. Serve with rolled cookies.

Serves 4

banana wraps

see variations page 278

A great speedy dessert using egg roll wrappers. Serve with a scoop of vanilla or caramel ice cream.

8 egg roll wrappers
2–3 bananas, sliced into 1/2-in. rounds
　(16 slices)
1 tsp. lemon juice

4 tsp. chocolate–hazelnut spread, divided
2 tbsp. melted sweet butter
1 tbsp. confectioners' sugar

Place 1 wrapper facing you like a diamond. Toss the bananas in lemon juice and put 4 banana slices in the center of the wrapper. Put chocolate–hazelnut spread on top. Turn in the pointed ends over the banana and roll up like a cigar. Brush all over with melted butter. Repeat with remaining wrappers.

Heat a skillet over medium heat and add the banana wraps. Cook until brown on the first side, about 4 minutes, then repeat on the second side. Dust with confectioner's sugar and serve immediately.

Serves 4

orange–berry cheesecake pie

see variations page 279

Having a ready-to-use pie shell in the pantry is to know that an impressive dessert is always at hand. This filling is quick and easy, and a surefire favorite.

juice and zest of 1 orange
3 tbsp. confectioners' sugar, divided
1 prepared pie shell
1 cup cream cheese

1 cup heavy cream or whipping cream
6 oz. blueberries, divided
4 oz. raspberries, divided
1/3 cup grape jelly, warmed

Combine 3 tablespoons of the orange juice and 1 tablespoon confectioners' sugar, and use to brush all over the pie shell to moisten and flavor.

Beat the cream cheese, orange zest, 1 tablespoon orange juice, and 2 tablespoons confectioners' sugar in a small bowl with an electric or hand mixer until smooth. In a separate bowl, beat the cream until it forms soft peaks; do not overbeat. Fold into the cream cheese mixture. Add all but 2 tablespoons of the blueberries. Spread this mixture over the prepared pie shell. Pile the raspberries and the remaining blueberries on top of the cream mixture. Brush with warmed grape jelly to glaze.

Serves 6–8

mini pancakes
with honeyed peaches

see variations page 280

Don't reserve pancakes for breakfast — they make a fabulous quick dessert or an after-school snack. Serve with vanilla ice cream for an indulgence.

1 cup all-purpose flour
1 tsp. baking powder
1/4 tsp. salt
1 egg
1/4 cup honey, divided

3 tbsp. butter, divided
1/2 cup milk
1 tbsp. lemon juice
4 ripe peaches, pitted and cut into slices

Preheat a broiler to medium high.

Sift the flour, baking powder, and salt into a bowl. Make a well in the center and break in the egg, 1 tablespoon honey, and 1 tablespoon melted butter. Beat, gradually adding the flour and the milk until you have a thick, creamy batter the consistency of heavy cream.

Mix remaining honey with the lemon juice. Lay peaches flat side up in a broiler pan. Dot each peach with 1 teaspoon butter and brush with the honey–lemon mixture. Cook 5–7 minutes.

While the peaches are cooking, heat a lightly buttered skillet or griddle. Add generous tablespoons of the batter to the pan, leaving room for spreading. Cook for 1–2 minutes, until bubbles begin to appear on the surface of the pancakes. Turn and cook on the second side. Remove from the pan and keep warm while preparing the next batch of pancakes.
Serves 6

chocolate macadamia slice

see variations page 281

This one is calories on a plate, but as an occasional treat, it is a winner.

1 stick butter or hard margarine (low-fat soft
   margarine will not set)
2 tbsp. soft brown sugar
1/4 cup cocoa powder
3 tbsp. corn syrup
2 cups crushed graham crackers, peanut butter
   cookies, or vanilla wafers

1/2 cup macadamia nuts, roughly chopped
1/2 cup raisins

for the topping
8 oz. (8 squares) semisweet chocolate, optional

In a saucepan over medium low heat, melt the butter, sugar, cocoa powder, and syrup until the sugar crystals disappear. Stir in the crushed graham crackers or cookies, nuts, and raisins.

Line an 8-inch square pan with plastic wrap. Press the cookie mixture into the pan and flatten with the back of a spoon. If using the topping, melt the chocolate over a double boiler, then smooth over the cookie base. Mark into squares and set in the refrigerator.

Serves 9–12

instant exotic fruit crisp

see variations page 282

A healthy dessert that is full of tropical flavors — great after a heavy meal or wonderfully refreshing on a hot day. As a timesaver, look for prepared fruit in the produce section; otherwise, buy fresh, but add in extra prep time.

2 cups fresh mango chunks
2 cups fresh pineapple chunks
1/2 cup apricot nectar
1 tbsp. lemon juice
1 tbsp. maple syrup, optional

for the topping
1/2 cup pecans
1/4 cup toasted coconut flakes
1/4 cup pitted dates, rough chopped
1/4 tsp. ground cinnamon

Combine the mango and pineapple in individual bowls. Mix together the apricot nectar and the lemon juice; taste and sweeten with maple syrup, if desired. Pour over the fruit bowls.

Combine all the ingredients for the topping in a food processor and pulse until the mixture is coarsely chopped. Scatter the mixture over the fruit.

Serves 4

cinnamon bagel crisps

see variations page 283

These handy little crisps can be made from frozen and thawed bagels, or from some that are slightly past their best. They make a great homemade addition to a bowl of ice cream or yogurt.

2 plain, whole-wheat, or cinnamon–raisin
    bagels
butter-flavored cooking spray or 2 tbsp. melted
    butter

1 tbsp. brown sugar
1 tsp. cinnamon

Preheat oven to 350°F.

Halve each bagel crosswise into 2 crescents, then slice into 4 thin width-wise strips; put on a baking sheet. Spray the bagels with cooking spray or brush with melted butter. Sprinkle with the brown sugar and cinnamon.

Bake in the oven until golden, about 10 minutes, then turn over and bake on the second side for 5–7 minutes. Be aware when cooking that thinner slices may cook slightly quicker than thicker slices. Serve warm or cold.

Serves 4

variations

crispy apricot toasts

see base recipe page 255

crispy ginger plum toasts
Prepare the basic recipe, replacing the apricots and ground cinnamon with small plums and ground ginger.

lemon–honey apricot toasts
Prepare the basic recipe, replacing the sugar with thick honey. Sprinkle the apricots with lemon juice before brushing with honey.

pecan & apricot toasts
Prepare the basic recipe, sprinkling 1/4 cup finely chopped pecans over the buttered bread slices before adding the sugar.

crispy pineapple toasts
Prepare the basic recipe, replacing the apricots with 1 (20-ounce) can of drained pineapple chunks.

variations

spiced apple & cranberry tartlets

see base recipe page 257

spiced apple & cinnamon crepes
Prepare the basic recipe for the apples. Use to stuff 4 prepared and warmed crepes instead of the phyllo shells.

spiced peach & brandy tartlets
Prepare the basic recipe, replacing the apples and cranberries with peaches, and adding 1 teaspoon of lemon juice and 1 tablespoon of brandy.

spiced pear & raisin tartlets
Prepare the basic recipe, replacing the apples and cranberries with pears and raisins.

spiced apples with pork
Prepare the basic recipe, omitting the confectioners' sugar. Serve as a side to roast pork or grilled pork steaks.

chocolate cake mousse with cherries

see base recipe page 258

white chocolate mousse with raspberries
Prepare the basic recipe, replacing semisweet chocolate with white chocolate, and cherries with raspberries. Replace the almond extract with vanilla extract.

mocha chocolate mousse with chocolate cocoa beans
Prepare the basic recipe, adding 1 teaspoon of instant coffee dissolved in 1 teaspoon boiling water to the melted chocolate. Proceed as directed and replace cherries with chocolate cocoa beans to garnish.

orange chocolate mousse
Prepare the basic recipe, using an orange-flavored semisweet chocolate and replacing the almond extract with 1 teaspoon grated orange zest. Drizzle 2 tablespoons orange juice or orange-flavored liqueur over the chocolate muffin chunks. Grate orange chocolate for the garnish and top with slices of fresh orange.

light chocolate mousse
Prepare the basic recipe, using 2 egg whites and omitting the cream. Whisk the egg whites and sugar until stiff, blend in 1/3 of the chocolate, and stir until smooth. Gently fold in the remaining chocolate until just combined.

variations

cherry hot fudge sundaes

see base recipe page 259

hot fudge banana sundaes
Prepare the basic recipe, replacing the cherries with 2 bananas that have been sliced and dipped in lemon juice.

pears belle helene sundaes
Prepare the basic recipe, replacing the cherries with 2 large pears that have been quartered and dipped in lemon juice, or 1 (15-ounce) can pears. Use 1 scoop of chocolate ice cream and 1 scoop of vanilla ice cream per person.

brownies with cherries & hot fudge sauce
Prepare the basic recipe, omitting the whipped cream. Place 4 good-quality brownies in serving bowls. Top with the ice cream and the hot chocolate sauce.

cherry–coconut chocolate sundaes
Prepare the basic recipe, replacing the chocolate sauce with one made by combining 4 ounces semisweet chocolate, which has been melted in a double boiler, and 1/2 cup coconut milk, which has been brought just to a boil. Stir until smooth. Proceed as directed.

variations

jeweled persian yogurt parfaits

see base recipe page 260

jeweled gingered yogurt parfaits
Prepare the basic recipe, replacing the rosewater with 4 pieces of chopped stem ginger and 2 tablespoons of the syrup from the jar. Add honey to taste; you will need very little or none at all.

black & green grape hazelnut parfaits
Prepare the basic recipe, replacing the pomegranate with 4 ounces each of black and green grapes, halved and seeded. Replace the pistachios with hazelnuts.

jeweled granola yogurt parfaits
Prepare the basic recipe, putting 2 tablespoons granola into the base of each dish and adding a 2-tablespoon layer of granola in the middle as you construct the dessert.

jeweled mango parfaits
Prepare the basic recipe, omitting the rosewater. Reduce the yogurt to 1 cup and combine with 1 cup puréed mango. Add the honey to taste; you will need very little or none at all.

variations

mock berry brûlée

see base recipe page 263

mock lemon–berry brûlée
Prepare the basic recipe, omitting the vanilla pudding and Kahlua. Use heavy cream or whipping cream and increase the quantity to 1 1/2 cups. Beat as directed and stir in 1/2 cup lemon curd and 1 teaspoon grated lemon zest. Proceed as directed.

sour cream–vanilla berry brûlée
Prepare the basic recipe, replacing the pudding mix, whipping cream, and Kahlua with 1 cup sour cream or Greek-style yogurt. Flavor with 2 tablespoons confectioners' sugar and 1/2 teaspoon vanilla extract.

mock cappuccino–pear brûlée
Prepare the basic recipe, replacing the berries with 2 large pears that have been quartered and dipped in lemon juice, or 1 (15-ounce) can pears. Dissolve 1 tablespoon instant coffee in 1 teaspoon hot water; cool. Add to the pudding mix and proceed as directed.

butterscotch brûlée pie
Prepare the basic recipe, but instead of berries, place 1 cup butterscotch chips in the base of a prepared pie crust. Prepare the crème as for basic recipe and spread over the crust. Sprinkle with brown sugar and caramelize as directed.

variations

banana wraps

see base recipe page 264

maple–pecan banana wraps
Prepare the basic recipe, replacing half of lemon juice and
chocolate–hazelnut spread with 2 tablespoons maple syrup and 1/4 cup
chopped pecans.

banana–marshmallow wraps
Prepare the basic recipe, replacing the chocolate–hazelnut spread with
2 tablespoons marshmallow paste or mini marshmallows.

banana–marmalade wraps
Prepare the basic recipe, replacing the chocolate–hazelnut spread with
2 tablespoons orange marmalade.

banana–cranberry wraps
Prepare the basic recipe, replacing the chocolate–hazelnut spread with
2 tablespoons cranberry sauce.

variations

orange–berry cheesecake pie

see base recipe page 266

lemon–berry cheesecake pie
Prepare the basic recipe, replacing orange juice with 2 tablespoons lemon juice to brush the pie shell. Spread 1/2 cup lemon curd over the base of the shell. For the cream cheese mixture, replace the orange zest and juice with lemon.

orange–strawberry cheesecake pie
Prepare the basic recipe, replacing the raspberries and blueberries with 8 ounces strawberries. Finely chop about a third of the strawberries into the cream mixture; pile the remainder on top.

cherry & kirsch cheesecake pie
Prepare the basic recipe, replacing the berries with 1 (20-ounce) jar of sweet cherries in syrup. Brush the inside of the pie shell with 2 tablespoons cherry juice mixed with 2 tablespoons kirsch; omit sugar. Pile the drained cherries on top of the shell. Boil remaining cherry syrup with 2 tablespoons kirsch till thick, and use to glaze the cherries. (If cherries are bottled in alcohol, omit kirsch.)

chocolate–raspberry cheesecake pie
Prepare the basic recipe, omitting blueberries. To the cream cheese mixture add 3 ounces melted and cooled semisweet chocolate. Top with 8 ounces raspberries, glaze, and garnish with grated chocolate, curls, or chocolate chips.

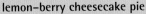

desserts 279

mini pancakes with honeyed peaches

see base recipe page 267

mini pancakes with cardamom honeyed plums
Prepare the basic recipe, replacing the peaches with 6 halved and sliced plums, and adding 1 teaspoon ground green cardamom seeds to the honey–lemon mixture.

mini pancakes with blueberries & lemon maple syrup
Prepare the basic recipe, omitting the peaches. Warm the juice of 1 lemon with 1/2 cup maple syrup; add 4 ounces blueberries and warm through. Serve drizzled over the pancakes.

mini pancakes with marmalade sauce
Prepare the basic recipe, omitting the peaches. Warm 2/3 cup marmalade with 2 tablespoons of orange juice or orange-flavored liqueur. Serve drizzled over the pancakes.

stuffed peaches
Omit the pancakes and omit the butter filling for the peaches. Instead, stuff the peaches with a mixture made from crumbling 6 small amoretti or macaroon cookies and 2 ounces of ricotta or cream cheese. Brush with honey–lemon mixture and cook as directed.

chocolate macadamia slice

see base recipe page 269

rocky road slice
Prepare the basic recipe, replacing the macadamia nuts and raisins with
1/3 cup mini marshmallows, 1/3 cup white chocolate chips, and 1/3 cup
peanut halves.

chocolate–cherry almond slice
Prepare the basic recipe, replacing the macadamia nuts and raisins with
candied cherries and chopped blanched almonds.

chocolate–apricot amoretti slice
Prepare the basic recipe, replacing the cookies, macadamia nuts, and raisins
with crushed amoretti cookies, apricots, and chopped blanched almonds.

chocolate, coconut & cranberry slice
Prepare the basic recipe, replacing the macadamia nuts and raisins with flaked
coconut and dried cranberries.

variations

instant exotic fruit crisp

see base recipe page 270

citrus crisp
Prepare the basic recipe, replacing the mango and pineapple with 3 oranges and 1 pink grapefruit. Grate 1 teaspoon of orange zest and add to the topping mixture. Peel the remaining oranges and grapefruit; cut into slices.

exotic fruit crisp with gingered cream
Prepare the basic recipe, adding a generous pinch of ground ginger with the cinnamon. For the cream, beat 1 cup whipping cream until soft peaks form, and add 4 finely chopped pieces of stem ginger and 2 teaspoons of stem ginger syrup from the jar.

exotic fruit crisp with honey–lemon yogurt
Prepare the basic recipe, replacing the maple syrup with honey. Flavor 1 cup yogurt with 2–3 tablespoons honey, 1 teaspoon grated lemon zest, and 1 tablespoon lemon juice.

berry crisp parfait
Prepare the basic recipe, replacing the mango and pineapple with 2 cups mixed berries. Layer the berries, nut crisp topping, and 1 cup vanilla yogurt in wine glasses.

variations

cinnamon bagel chips

see base recipe page 271

apple bagel chips
Prepare the basic recipe. Shred the flesh of a peeled and cored Granny Smith
apple and mix with 1 tablespoon lemon juice. Spread thinly on the bagels and
top with the sugar and cinnamon.

bagel crisps with chocolate-hazelnut drizzle
Prepare the basic recipe, omitting the cinnamon. Drizzle 1/4 cup warmed
chocolate-hazelnut spread over the plate of finished bagels.

sesame bagel chips
Prepare the basic recipe, spraying the bagels as directed. Replace the sugar and
cinnamon with 1 teaspoon salt and 1 tablespoon sesame seeds.

italian bagel chips
Prepare the basic recipe. Spray the bagels as directed, replacing the cooking
spray or butter with olive oil. Replace the sugar and cinnamon with 1 teaspoon
sea salt, a generous grinding of black pepper, 1 teaspoon dried Italian herbs,
and 1 tablespoon shredded Parmesan cheese.

index